Presented to:

_____

Presented by:

_____

Date:

_____

E-MAIL FROM GOD
FOR GRADS

E-MAIL FROM GOD
FOR GRADS

by

Claire Cloninger & Curt Cloninger

RIVER
OAK
PUBLISHING

Tulsa, Oklahoma

E-mail from God for Grads
ISBN 1-58919-942-1
46-117-00003
Copyright © 2002 by Claire Cloninger & Curt Cloninger
Represented by: Alive Communications, Inc.
7680 Goddard Street
Colorado Springs, CO 80920

Published by RiverOak Publishing
P.O. Box 700143
Tulsa, Oklahoma 74170-0143

I'M TAKING THIS TRIP WITH YOU!

Have I not commanded you? Be strong and courageous.
Do not be terrified; do not be discouraged, for the
LORD your God will be with you wherever you go."

| | Joshua | 1:9 | |

Dear Child,

>Graduation is a big step—I realize that. In a way it's like walking through a door into a different life. The things that are expected of you will be different. Your new school or job will have new rules. You may be moving away from your parents' home. New places and situations don't stop me, though. I'm planning to make this trip with you. Remember, I made you a promise, and I intend to keep it. I promised to be with you wherever you go. You don't have to pack me in your suitcase. You don't have to strap me in a seat belt in the car. You don't have to enroll me in your college.

I'll be with you—in your heart, your mind, your spirit, your conscience. I'll be whispering words of encouragement and giving you my guidance when you get confused. Be strong! Don't be afraid! You've got a friend.

Your Father,
>God

== == ==   == == == == == == == == ==

USE YOUR GIFTS CREATIVELY

Make a careful exploration of who you are and the work you have been given, and then sink yourself into that. Don't be impressed with yourself. Don't compare yourself with others. Each of you must take responsibility for doing the creative best you can with your own life.

Galatians 6:4-5   THE MESSAGE

My Child,

>I guess you've noticed that I didn't crank out a world of clones. Even if you looked in every city and town on the planet, you would never find another person exactly like you. You are an original, inside and out.

Part of your assignment as My child is to get to know yourself—what you're good at and what you like. This isn't a competition between you and anyone else. I don't grade on the curve. Be confident—you have a right to be. You're awesome!

Let Me help you discover how to use the gifts I've given you, performing work that you find exciting. I want to see your life count for something great!

Your Creator,
>God

== == ==   == == == == == == == == ==

TO LOVE IS TO OBEY

**The world must learn that I love the Father and that
I do exactly what my Father has commanded me.**

| | | John | | 14:31 | | | | |

Dear Child,

>My Son, Jesus, perfectly obeyed Me. If I told Him to pray for twelve
hours, He did. If I told Him not to eat or drink for forty days, He didn't.
Why did He obey Me? Because He loved Me. Until you love Me,
obeying Me seems like a great big pain. When you love Me, you'll
want to do what I command.

How do you learn to love Me? Start by receiving My love for you.
Once you realize how much I love you, that I sacrificed My Son just to
be with you, that I have wonderful plans for your life, and that I am
proud of you, you'll want to love Me back. Once you love Me, obeying
Me won't be a painful duty; it will be a joy.

Your Loving Father,
>God

== == ==   == == == == == == == == ==

PRESCRIPTION FOR A GOOD LIFE

Whoever wants to embrace life and see the day fill up with good, Here's what you do: Say nothing evil or hurtful; Snub evil and cultivate good; run after peace for all you're worth.

| 1 Peter 3:10-11 | THE MESSAGE |

Dear Child,

>Want a prescription for a good life? I've got one, but don't expect anything supernatural. It's plain old common sense. Here it is: Don't run off at the mouth with harmful gossip and mindless chatter. You can hurt other people with your words.

When you see your friends headed for trouble, turn around and run in the other direction. It's not worth being part of the crowd if the crowd is getting ready to jump off a cliff. It doesn't take a rocket scientist to figure out that reckless, dangerous choices lead to a reckless, dangerous life.

Run away from what's bad for you, and run after what's good. You'll be rewarding yourself with peace and happiness, and your regrets will be few. Trust Me!

The Author of Common Sense,
>God

== == ==   == == == == == == == == ==

IT'S OKAY, YOUR DADDY'S HERE

Comfort, comfort my people, says your God.

Isaiah 40:1

My Child,

>Have you ever seen a little kid slip and skin a knee? Hopefully, a parent is nearby to scoop up that child and say, "Daddy's here," or, "Mommy's here. It's okay." The older a child gets, the more society says it's not okay to cry. Teenagers are supposed to act cool. Adults are supposed to hide their hurts.

The problem is, everyone still gets hurt and wants to be comforted. Because people are conditioned to act like they're fine when they're not, they are full of hidden wounds and silent tears. I want you to know that I see your pain and I care. I am waiting to scoop you up and comfort you. I'm waiting to say, "It's okay, your Daddy's here."

Your Comforter,
>God

== == ==   == == == == == == == == ==

IT'S NOT WHAT YOU KNOW

Knowledge puffs up, but love builds up.

| 1 Corinthians | 8:1 |

Dear Child,

>Would I rather you know a bunch of things, or would I rather you love people? What do you think? Knowing lots of information is fine, but if all it does is make you conceited, what good is it? You can't impress Me with what you know. Lots of people know lots of things about Me, but where are the people who will love in My name?

Look at the heroes of the Bible. What did they know? Peter was a plain fisherman, the prophet Amos was a farmer, and John the Baptist preached in the desert and ate locusts and wild honey. Even Jesus was a carpenter. It doesn't take a college degree to please Me. If you encourage, help, and care about other people, that impresses Me.

Your Encourager,
>God

== == ==   == == == == == == == == ==

I'LL MAKE A WAY

I will lead the blind by ways they have not known, along unfamiliar paths I will guide them; I will turn the darkness into light before them and make the rough places smooth. These are the things I will do; I will not forsake them.

| Isaiah | 42:16 |

Dear Child,

>Do you ever feel like you're caught in a game of blindman's bluff, stumbling blindfolded through life, never quite sure whether you're getting ready to run into a brick wall or step off of a high cliff? I don't want you to feel alone in the dark. I'm right here with you.

When you have to make a hard decision and you're in the dark about what to do, I'll shine My light on the situation so the answer will be clear. When you see everyone else headed down a dark, dead-end alley, stop! Don't go there! I'll be the light that leads you in the right direction. When you feel unpopular for taking a stand and the going gets rough, I'll show up to smooth the path under your feet. Trust Me. I'll make a way for you.

The Pathfinder,
>God

== == ==   == == == == == == == == ==

YOU ARE GIFTED FOR A REASON

Be generous with the different things God gave you, passing them around so all get in on it.

🖨️ 📎 ✝️ ♡ ▼ | 1 Peter 4:10 | THE MESSAGE ▼ | ✉️ ✋ 📖 📋

Dear Child,

>Ever think of the billions of people I've already made and wonder why I needed you? Is there a real purpose for your life? Trust Me, I gave every person special gifts—you included. Maybe you haven't found yours yet, but you will.

Some people are good managers. Some are good artists, athletes, teachers, or writers. I designed all people so their gifts would work to benefit others. The problem is, many people don't care two cents about anybody else. They use whatever talents they've got to make a better life for themselves. I hope you won't see things that way. Let Me help you discover your gifts and show you how to share them. You are gifted for a reason!

Your Creator,
>God

== == ==   == == == == == == == == ==

GUARD THE SPRING OF YOUR HEART

**Watch over your heart with all diligence,
for from it flow the springs of life.**

| Proverbs | 4:23 NASB |

Dear Child,

>Let Me tell you a story. Once there was a child who drank every day from a bubbling spring. Because the spring water was pure, the child grew to be healthy and strong. Then one day while she was off playing, her enemy came and put a few drops of poison in the spring. That's all it took. Not knowing of the poison, the child continued to drink the water daily, and gradually, she began to feel sick and sad.

Now let Me explain. The spring is your heart where your thoughts and emotions live. Satan is your enemy who wants to poison your heart with his lies. When you trust Me, I'll pour My truth into your heart, washing away Satan's lies. I'll also help you build a wall around the spring to guard your heart.

Your Gatekeeper,
>God

== == ==   == == == == == == == == ==

DON'T GIVE UP

**Let's not allow ourselves to get fatigued doing good.
At the right time we will harvest a good crop if we don't give up.**

| Galatians 6:9 | THE MESSAGE |

My Child,

>Sometimes the temptation to quit is overwhelming. When you feel beat and burned out, it seems like nobody cares whether you keep trying or not. Well, there's something I want you to hear loud and clear. I care! Never forget that for a minute.

In the midst of all your challenges, I'm with you. Life is a big tug-of-war between the call to care about others and to do good, and the temptation to quit. Quitting says that nothing matters and life is a throwaway. When you hang in there and "keep on keeping on," you affirm My call on your life to make a difference.

So, dig in, and stand up. I've got you covered, and I won't let you go. Don't give up! I love you.

Your Encourager,
>God

== == ==   == == == == == == == == ==

STOP WORRYING AND WAIT

Wait for the LORD; be strong and take heart and wait for the LORD.

| Psalm | 27:14 |

Dear Child,

>Have you ever heard of the serenity prayer? It's not in the Bible, but it's still a pretty good prayer. "God, grant me the serenity to accept the things I cannot change, the courage to change the things I can, and the wisdom to know the difference." When you've done everything you can to change your situation, and it still hasn't changed, you have two choices: 1. Keep banging your head against the wall, spinning your wheels, worrying, laboring, and failing; or 2. Wait for me.

Waiting doesn't mean giving up. You can still pray and listen while you wait. You can even be strong and hopeful while you wait. The truth is, you can't control everything that happens to you. If you could, you'd be God, and I'd be out of a job. Your job is to trust me, and I will give you my peace and be with you while you wait.

Your Serenity,
>God

== == ==   == == == == == == == == ==

I WANT TO AMAZE YOU

**Call to me and I will answer you and tell you
great and unsearchable things you do not know.**

| Jeremiah | 33:3 |

Dear Child of Mine,

>Part of the fun of being God is blowing people's minds. I'm serious! I know everything, and every now and then, I'll share something deep with one of My children. I love watching their eyes pop open as the light goes off in their heads and they say, "Wow, I get it!"

I have some of those eye-opening revelations that I want to share with you. I've created you to understand and appreciate things about Me that no one else will ever know. I want to share it with you and only you. Spend time with Me and call on Me. Read My Book. Then listen and prepare to be amazed.

Your Maker,
>God

== == ==   == == == == == == == == ==

IT'S NOT ALL ABOUT MONEY

You cannot serve both God and Money.

| Matthew | 6:24 |

My Child,

>Do you trust Me to take care of you, or do you trust in your money? If you go to college, get a high-paying job, and have a large house and a fancy car, will that protect you from any problems? No. Things go wrong, even for rich people. Money can't protect you from everything.

I *can* protect you—whether you have money or not. I control all the money in the world. I own everything. It's My world, so why not rely on Me instead of money. I can give you the money you need, or I can just give you the things you need without you even having to spend money on them. The point is that I can take care of you. If you trust in money to take care of you, eventually it will let you down.

Your Provider,
>God

== == ==   == == == == == == == == ==

WILL YOU GO?

In you the fatherless find compassion.

Hosea	14:3

My Child,

>In the streets of Calcutta, India, right now, a twelve-year-old girl begs for food. She has no parents. She is sick and malnourished. She has been sexually abused so many times it seems normal to her. She is just one of literally millions of parentless street children in the cities of the world. Where will she find compassion?

Why am I telling you this? Because there are hurting people all around. Seek Me as to your role—how you are to get involved, and with whom and where. Perhaps I want to bless you financially to help send missionaries to the field. Perhaps you want to get involved in a more direct way. Certainly you can pray. Let's spend some time together so that I can share My will for your life. Whatever your role is in My work, I promise it will be more fun than you ever dreamed. As in all giving, you will receive back far more than you are capable of giving.

The Father of All,
>God

== == ==   == == == == == == == == ==

CLONINGER

TALK IS CHEAP

**All hard work brings a profit, but
mere talk leads only to poverty.**

Proverbs 14:23

Dear Child,

>Have you heard the saying, "Put your money where your mouth is"?
It means, "Stop talking and do something about it." Everybody has
ideas, but not everybody acts on those ideas. Lots of people had
ideas for computer programs in the 1970s, but Bill Gates didn't just
talk about writing computer programs, he sold his computer programs
to IBM.

It's not the talkers who succeed, it's the doers. The same is true
when it comes to following Me. Anybody can sit around and talk
about how much they love Me, but the people who impress Me are
the ones who take action. So tell people about Me, write songs to
Me, and work for Me. Anybody can say they love Me, but will you do
something about it?

Your Motivation,
>God

== == ==   == == == == == == == == ==

IF YOU REALLY LOOK, YOU'LL FIND ME

You will seek me and find me when you seek me with all your heart.

Jeremiah 29:13

Dear Child of Mine,

>Have you ever lost something that you didn't really expect to find again? Sure, you rummaged around the house looking for it, but since you didn't actually think you'd ever find it, you didn't really look with much hope or expectation. You know what happens in those situations? Since you don't expect to find it, you rarely do.

Some people look for Me like that. "Oh, God's out there, but He's so far above me, I'll never reach Him." Believe Me when I say that if you'll put your heart into looking for Me, you will find Me! I am so close to you. Open the eyes of your heart and really look. Expect Me to be here, because here I am.

Your Friend,
>God

== == ==   == == == == == == == == ==

MY FORGIVENESS IS RADICAL

**I, even I, am he who blots out your transgressions,
for my own sake, and remembers your sins no more.**

| Isaiah | 43:25 |

Dear Child,

>Let Me show you how radical My forgiveness is. First of all, when you tell Me about the junk in your life and turn away from it, I immediately forgive you. That's step one. The next thing I do is blot out your sin. I take a big old sponge and soak up the stain of whatever you've done. It's like having a big blob of spaghetti sauce on your white tennis shoes one minute, and the next minute, you can't find a trace of the stain.

Wait, there's more! Not only do I blot up the stain, but once it's gone, I can't even remember that it was ever there! I develop amnesia about it, so please confess your junk and turn the other way. Then I'll do My part. I'll blot it out and forget it!

Your Forgiving Father,
>God

== == ==   == == == == == == == == ==

TAKE A CHANCE

We know and rely on the love God has for us.

| 1 John | 4:16 |

Dear Child,

>Have you ever gone hiking with a walking stick? It makes hiking a lot easier. You don't even have to lean on it all the time; just knowing it's there makes you more confident. With a walking stick, you will take risks on a steep trail that you wouldn't otherwise.

I want My love for you to be like that walking stick. I love you so much, and I will never stop loving you. I want you to know My love and rely on it. Just knowing that I love you should give you confidence to risk being rejected by people, because My love will catch you if they hurt you. You can afford to take chances. You can afford to love the unlovable. No matter what happens, you can never lose My love.

Your Support,
>God

== == ==   == == == == == == == == ==

JESUS MADE YOU INNOCENT

Therefore, there is now no condemnation for those who are in Christ Jesus, because through Christ Jesus the law of the Spirit of life set me free from the law of sin and death.

Romans   8:1-2

My Child,

>I want to talk to you about some deep stuff. Because My Son, Jesus, died for all your wrong thoughts, words, and actions, you're not guilty anymore. The devil still wants you to feel guilty, though, so he condemns you. In other words, he makes you feel bad about yourself for no specific reason.

Sometimes when you do something wrong, I'll cause you to feel bad about that one thing so you'll tell Me you're sorry, but I'll never make you feel bad about who you are. That's different. I love who you are, and if you've asked My Son to live in your heart, you'll feel My love.

I want you to be free from feeling bad about yourself and free from doing bad things. That's why Jesus died for you—to set you free! My love will always lift you up!

The Lord of Freedom,
>God

== == ==   == == == == == == == == ==

I KNOW YOU BETTER THAN YOU KNOW YOURSELF

**All a man's ways seem right to him,
but the LORD weighs the heart.**

| Proverbs | 21:2 |

Dear Child,

>Do you realize that you can think you're right and still be totally wrong? Have you ever argued, "The movie starts at seven o'clock, I'm sure of it!" And then you show up, and the movie has been on since six o'clock? Or maybe you've convinced yourself that you're being nice to someone for the right reasons, but really you're just being nice to them to copy their homework.

Whatever it is, you may fool yourself and others, but you can't fool Me. I can see right through to the core of your heart. I know when you're being honest, and when you're just lying to yourself. If you really want to know right from wrong, don't trust yourself. Trust Me. Trust My Bible. I'll never lie to you.

Your Conscience,
>God

== == ==   == == == == == == == == ==

HOW TO CHOOSE WELL

I will go to the king, even though it is
against the law. And if I perish, I perish.

Esther   4:16

Dear Child,

>Esther was a beautiful young Jewish woman who became the queen
of Persia, but her husband, the king, didn't know she was Jewish.
Esther found out that an evil man named Haman was plotting to have
all the Jews In the land put to death. She knew she had to tell the
king about the plot, but the penalty for approaching the king without
being summoned was death. Here was Esther's dilemma: Should she
risk death to save her people, or should she save her own neck and let
them die? Esther saved her people, and her own life was spared.

Like Esther, you'll have some important choices to make in your life—
choices that may be risky. Come to Me when you need the wisdom
and courage to choose well.

Your Counselor,
>God

== == ==   == == == == == == == == ==

IT'S A JUNGLE OUT THERE!

A righteous man may have many troubles,
but the Lord delivers him from them all.

| Psalm | 34:19 |

Dear Child,

>People are so confused about the way I work. They think My job is to get rid of all their troubles. I'm supposed to fix every bad situation and make every circumstance perfect.

Sorry. That's not My job. I will fix many of your circumstances, but you're still going to have some troubles. The good news is, as you get to know Me, you'll find that I am always with you. I will lead you through your troubles and out the other side.

Think of your life as a jungle, and me as your Guide. I'm not going to turn the whole jungle into Disneyland, but I will lead you *through* it. When your life gets wild, don't freak out. Just stick close, and we'll get through it together.

Your Guide,
>God

== == ==   == == == == == == == == ==

THINK DIFFERENT

"My thoughts are not your thoughts, neither are your ways my ways," declares the Lord. "As the heavens are higher than the earth, so are my ways higher than your ways and my thoughts than your thoughts."

Isaiah 55:8-9

Dear Child,

>If you can't figure me out, that's because I'm not like anybody you've ever known. I don't think the way you think. I don't just think "out of the box," I think miles above the box. Consequently, I will put you in some situations that make absolutely no sense to you. "Why do I have to take this philosophy class? I want to be a nurse?" "Why do I have to wait tables? I want to be a musician."

When I put you somewhere, and you have no idea why, that's when you have to trust me. I made you, and I'm preparing you for something great that you can't even imagine. Your life is not just for today. It's OK to ask, "Why, Lord?" But be willing to obey me, even when it seems crazy. I know what I'm doing. I just do things a little differently.

Your Unique Leader,
>God

== == ==   == == == == == == == == ==

WHAT DO YOU WANT ME TO DO FOR YOU?

"What do you want me to do for you?" Jesus asked him.
The blind man said, "Rabbi, I want to see." "Go," said
Jesus, "your faith has healed you." Immediately he
received his sight and followed Jesus along the road.

Mark | **10:51-52**

Dear Child,

>My Son has good manners. He would never push His way into your life, changing and rearranging everything, without your permission. He waits to be invited in, and then He waits to hear what you want.

"What do you want Me to do for you?" He asked a blind man, and the blind man answered, "Rabbi, I want to see." This man had enough faith to ask for what he wanted, so Jesus didn't fool around. He answered the blind man's request immediately, and the blind man regained his sight. More than that, he began to follow Jesus.

What do you want Jesus to do for you? Do you want to see Him? Believe in Him? That's one request He wants to answer. All you have to do is ask.

Your Father,
>God

== == ==   == == == == == == == == ==

WHAT WOULD THEY SAY?

Live a life of love.

| Ephesians | 5:2 |

My Child,

>If you died tonight, how would you be remembered? At your funeral, what would they say? Would they say, "That person loved to win," or, "That person really loved baseball"? Would they say, "Oh yeah, I think that person went to church once in a while"?

Or would it be different? Would someone stand up and say, "She was kind to me my first day at school. When everyone else ignored me, she asked me to sit with her at lunch. I'll always remember that." Will someone else say, "She always encouraged me to hang in there at track practice. I ran my best race because of her."

Are you living a life of love that is making a real difference, or are you living a life that hardly matters? When everything else fades away, the love you show to others is what will last. So live a life of love.

The One Who Loves You,
>God

== == ==   == == == == == == == == ==

JESUS IS THE DOOR TO ME

"I am the door; if anyone enters through Me, he will be saved, and shall go in and out and find pasture."

| John | 10:9 NASB |

Dear Child,

>There is a door that leads directly to My heart. It's not hidden or hard to find. I have made sure that it's right out in plain sight so nobody can miss it. What is this door I'm talking about? My Son, Jesus, is the door that leads to Me, and He's wide open for you to come through. He's closer than your heartbeat—always just a prayer away.

Faith in Jesus is the path that leads through the door into My love, mercy, strength, and the answers you need. Pray in the name of Jesus. Look for the will of Jesus. Put everything in the hands of Jesus, and you'll find yourself inside My pasture where the flock of My family gets fed. What are you waiting for? Come in and chow down!

Your Father,
>God

== == ==   == == == == == == == == ==

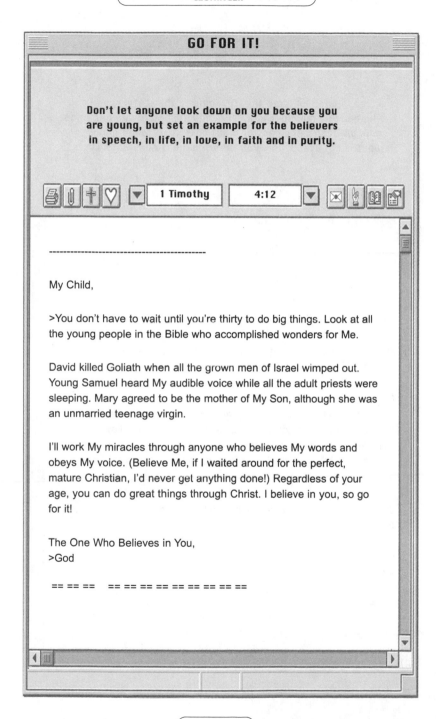

GO FOR IT!

Don't let anyone look down on you because you are young, but set an example for the believers in speech, in life, in love, in faith and in purity.

1 Timothy 4:12

My Child,

>You don't have to wait until you're thirty to do big things. Look at all the young people in the Bible who accomplished wonders for Me.

David killed Goliath when all the grown men of Israel wimped out. Young Samuel heard My audible voice while all the adult priests were sleeping. Mary agreed to be the mother of My Son, although she was an unmarried teenage virgin.

I'll work My miracles through anyone who believes My words and obeys My voice. (Believe Me, if I waited around for the perfect, mature Christian, I'd never get anything done!) Regardless of your age, you can do great things through Christ. I believe in you, so go for it!

The One Who Believes in You,
>God

== == ==   == == == == == == == == ==

THE BEST FOOD IS FREE

Come, all you who are thirsty, come to the waters; and you who have no money, come, buy and eat! Come, buy wine and milk without money and without cost. Why spend money on what is not bread, and your labor on what does not satisfy?

Isaiah 55:1-2

Dear Child,

>A lot of people think that becoming a child of God requires following a bunch of impossible religious rules. "Yeah," they grumble, "I would live for God, but He doesn't want me. I can't be good enough anyway." *What a lie!*

Most free stuff is crummy; but My free gift of Heaven, where you will live in joy for eternity, is the most valuable present you'll ever receive. All you have to do to get to Heaven is to believe in and follow My Son, Jesus. To have My power in your life, you just need to let Jesus sit in the driver's seat and take control of your life. That's it! Simple, isn't it?

Stop buying the moldy bread of this world, and come feast on My love for you. It's free!

Your Host,
>God

== == ==   == == == == == == == == ==

WE MAKE A GREAT TEAM!

Do not fear, for I am with you; do not be dismayed,
for I am your God. I will strengthen you and help you;
I will uphold you with my righteous right hand.

| Isaiah | 41:10 |

My Child,

>In sports, it's fun to be on a good team. That way, when you go out against a tough opponent, the strong players on your side increase your chances of winning. Trusting your life to Me puts you on the most powerful team in the universe. You are lining up at the 50-yard line alongside Me, My Son, and My Holy Spirit, not to mention an enormous host of angels and all the saints who have gone before you! Trust Me, you're on the winning side! I'm not bragging—that's just the way it is.

Here's My advice to you today: Don't be afraid and never give up, no matter how bad things look. I am your God. I'm here to help you. I'm here to hold you up when you feel like throwing in the towel and quitting. Go on—get in the game, and when things get tough, remember that I'm on your side!

The Ultimate Athlete,
>God

== == ==   == == == == == == == == ==

TURN AROUND AND SEE ME HERE

I am the LORD; that is my name! I will not give my glory to another or my praise to idols.

| Isaiah | 42:8 |

Dear Child,

>If you could catch a glimpse of how much I love you, it would change you. If you could see the consuming fire of My love, it would shock you. You'd turn around and look at Me and there would be no words to express your amazement. I am the Lord—that's who I am. I long for a relationship with you that is more real, more honest, and more powerful than any other relationship in your life. I have so much to share with you. I don't want you to get so tangled up in the cheap stuff that you're blind to Me.

Think about it. Is there anything you've made a little god out of? Is there something so important to you that it's coming between us? Don't let anything else take center place in your heart. Turn around and see Me here.

I Am the Lord,
>God

== == ==   == == == == == == == == ==

GOD DON'T MAKE NO JUNK

As for God, his way is perfect;
the word of the Lord is flawless.

Psalm **18:30**

Dear Child,

>You grow up expecting your parents to be perfect, and when you first realize that they're not, it's disappointing. After all, you trusted them. They taught you everything. They had all the answers.

As the saying goes, however, "nobody's perfect"—except Me. I have never made a mistake, and I never will. Do you think giraffes were a mistake? Think again. I made them, and I'm perfect. Everything I do and say is perfect.

Do you think you're a mistake? No way! Remember, I don't make mistakes. I made you exactly the way you are for a reason. Stick with Me, and I'll show you why I'm so proud of you.

Your Creator,
>God

== == ==   == == == == == == == == ==

I SEE YOUR TEARS

**"Blessed are those who mourn,
for they will be comforted."**

| | | Matthew | | 5:4 | | | |

My Child,

>Is it good to be sad? Well, it depends on what you're sad about. If you're sad because you didn't get the latest video game for Christmas, you'll just have to get over it. What if you're sad because of something more serious? Did a relative die? Do your friends reject you? Do you feel empty inside because someone has seriously hurt you? If so, then yes, you can be blessed by My comforting presence.

If your heart is breaking, My Spirit is with you. I know what's making you sad. I want to make it better. Cry out to Me. Pour your heart out to Me. Ask Me to help you. I will pick you up, dry your tears, and hold you. I will tell you that I love you. I promise I will be with you always.

Your Comforter,
>God

== == ==   == == == == == == == == ==

TURN ON YOUR HEADLIGHTS

**Your word is a lamp to my feet
and a light for my path.**

| Psalm | 119:105 |

Dear Child,

>Have you ever tried to find your way down a path in the dark without a flashlight? You can't make a whole lot of progress, can you? You stumble over every bump in the road. You can't even be sure if you're headed in the right direction. For all you know, you could be going around in circles.

Trying to make it through life without the light of My Word is like that. It's like asking to get lost—like signing up for a lifetime of bumps and detours and wrong turns. Reading My Word is like turning on your headlights. Suddenly, you are able to see clearly! Even though you can't see where the road ends, you'll be able to see where you are and how to get there. So pick up My Word and turn on the lights.

The Headlights of Your Life,
>God

== == ==   == == == == == == == == ==

BE A JANITOR

**"He who is least among you all—
he is the greatest."**

| Luke | 9:48 |

My Child,

>Titles, accomplishments, and awards don't impress Me. As a matter
of fact, I'm often more impressed by the heart of the janitor than I am
by the president of a company. People at the top sometimes *use*
others instead of *serving others.*

If you're a janitor, however, whom are you going to use? As a janitor,
you're always serving others. You have to come to work every day
willing to clean up other people's messes. It's that type of serving that
impresses Me. My Son could have come to earth as a king or
president, but He came as a servant.

When I see someone willing to serve others, I'll put them on top,
because I know I can trust them.

Your Servant,
>God

== == ==   == == == == == == == == ==

YOU CAN WALK ON WATER, TOO

"Come," he said. Then Peter got down out of the boat, walked on the water and came toward Jesus.

| Matthew | 14:29 |

Dear Child,

>One day Jesus wanted to spend some time alone praying, so He sent His friends ahead of Him in a boat to cross the Sea of Galilee. When it got dark, the wind started howling and the sea got rough. Suddenly, they saw Jesus walking toward them on the water. All of them were majorly spooked, thinking He was a ghost! So He called out, "Don't worry, guys. It's just Me." That's when Peter said, "If it's You, let me come to You." So Jesus said, "Come on," and Peter found out how it felt to walk on water. The only time he started to sink was when he took his eyes off of Jesus and looked at the storm.

Here's the lesson for you. Don't get focused on the rough winds of your circumstances. Keep your eyes on Jesus, and He'll hold you up!

His Father and Yours,
>God

== == ==   == == == == == == == == ==

DON'T EXPECT A PARADE

Consider him who endured such opposition from sinful men, so that you will not grow weary and lose heart.

| Hebrews | 12:3 |

My Child,

>When you stand up for what's right, some people aren't going to like it. My Son, Jesus, stood against greed when He drove the merchants out of the temple, and the merchants hated Him for cutting into their profits. Jesus stood against prejudice when He ate at a tax collector's house, and the prejudiced religious people hated Him for it.

When you are good to others, the people who are mean aren't going to like you much, because your good behavior is a criticism of their bad behavior. Don't let that stop you. Later, some of your enemies may admire your courage and change their minds. Don't expect everyone to shout for joy because you're following Me, though. That's okay. Don't take it personally. Plenty of people didn't like Jesus either. It comes with the territory.

Your Encourager,
>God

== == ==   == == == == == == == == ==

MY NAME MEANS "PROVIDER"

Abraham called that place The Lord Will Provide. And to this day it is said, "On the mountain of the Lord it will be provided."

Genesis	22:14

Dear Child,

>One of My most powerful names is "Jehovah-Jireh," which means "Provider." It means that I am the God who provides for My children. A long time ago, Abraham learned a lesson about My provision—a lesson he never forgot. Abraham was willing to sacrifice his son, but I provided a ram instead. Abraham learned that although I sometimes test, I also provide.

That's true for you, too. Whatever the circumstances or the situation— in trials, in temptation, in tests—keep your eyes open for My provision, and you'll find it there. Look for Me in the midst of your hardest times, and you'll find Me there, providing whatever you need—wisdom, strength, hope, and faith.

Your Provider,
>God

== == ==   == == == == == == == == ==

I WROTE THE BOOK OF YOUR LIFE

All the days ordained for me were written in your book before one of them came to be.

| Psalm | 139:16 |

Dear Child,

>Have you ever seen a movie based on a book that you've already read? Even during the most tense parts of the movie, you're not worried, because you know how it's going to turn out. Well, not only have I read the book of your life, I wrote the book of your life. You may be wondering, "How will this turn out?" but I'm not wondering.

There's an old song that says, "Many things about tomorrow I don't seem to understand. But I know who holds tomorrow, and I know who holds my hand."

I encourage you to take my hand and let me lead you into the future.

When your life seems scary and uncertain, come to me and let me calm you down. Take my hand and trust me. Remember, I wrote the book.

Your Author,
>God

== == == == == == == == == == == ==

WHAT DOES IT MEAN?

Carrying his own cross, he went out to the pace of the Skull (which in Aramaic is calle Golgotha). Here they crucified him, and with him two others—one on each side and Jesus in the middle.

John   19:17-18

Dear Child,

>Have you noticed how many people wear a cross as jewelry? You see cross necklaces and cross earrings—gold ones and silver ones, plain ones and fancy ones. In fact, crosses are such common accessories that we rarely stop to think of what they signify.

To the people of Jesus' day, wearing a cross as a decoration would be about like you wearing a little electric chair on a chain around your neck or little electric chairs dangling from your ears! It was not a shiny ornament you could hold in the palm of your hand. It was a rough, heavy instrument of torture that Jesus had to carry on His own back. It was a dreaded device of death to which He was nailed. It cost Him everything.

Now it is a symbol of victory! The cross is empty because Jesus rose from the dead and is seated at My right hand in Heaven. It's a symbol that means everything to Me.

Your Father,
>God

== == ==   == == == == == == == == ==

GOD LOVES A WORKER

Jesus said to them, "My Father is always at his work to this very day, and I, too, am working."

| John | 5:17 |

My Child,

>I am a working guy. I built the world in six days. I took one day off to rest, and I've been working ever since. My Son, Jesus, is also a working man. He worked as a carpenter for years, and then He became the hardest-working preacher and teacher ever. Jesus and I are still at work. We haven't stopped.

Day and night, I am at work introducing Myself to people who don't know Me. I control the course of governments. I keep the planets spinning. I work through Christians, doing miracles, healing hearts, and bringing joy into the world. Will you join in and work with Me? You won't have to do the miracles yourself. I will work them through you. You just have to be willing to pray for the people I show to you. If you're interested, pray right now, "Yes, Lord, I will work with You." Then keep your eyes open for your next job assignment.

Your Heavenly Boss,
>God

== == ==   == == == == == == == == ==

GET WISE

**Those who have insight among the people
will give understanding to the many.**

| | Daniel | 11:33 NASB | |

Dear Child,

>The more you hang out with Me, the wiser you become. My wisdom
points out solutions to problems and helps you make good choices.
It's like you've been walking around in a fog, and when you start
following Me, the fog lifts, and you see clearly.

Why do I give you wisdom, insight, and understanding? To help you
take the right road? Sure! That's one of the reasons, but it's more
than that. When I make one of My kids wise, I also do it so they can
help others who are still walking around in a fog. How do you help?
Not by being pushy or acting like a big know-it-all, but by being a
friend, praying for others, and allowing Me to show you quiet ways to
share your faith. Trust Me. I will guide you.

The Wisdom Giver,
>God

== == ==   == == == == == == == == ==

I'M STRONG TO THE FINISH

I love you, O LORD, my strength.

Psalm 18:1

My Dear Child,

>Where would Popeye have been without his spinach? He'd have been toast. Brutus was ten times bigger than Popeye; but as long as Popeye could reach his spinach, Brutus didn't stand a chance.

I'm your spinach. I'm your strength. I guarantee that there are things in life that you aren't strong enough to handle. Don't beat yourself up about it. Come to Me and pray for strength. I can make your mind strong. I can even give your body supernatural strength to keep going. I can make your heart strong when it feels like breaking. I can make your will strong when you feel like giving up. When you're feeling weak, simply pray, "Help me, God." It's not cheating to rely on Me. I want to help you.

Your Strength,
>God

== == ==   == == == == == == == == ==

STICK TO WHAT YOU KNOW

God is our refuge and strength, an ever-present help in trouble. Therefore we will not fear, though the earth give way and the mountains fall into the heart of the sea, though its waters roar and foam and the mountains quake with their surging.

Psalm 46:1-3

Dear Child,

>There have always been people in every age who have spread the rumor that the sky is falling or that the end of the world is coming next Thursday. When Jesus was asked to pinpoint the end of time, He made it clear that no one would know when it was coming.

So why should you get all bogged down in what you don't know? I'd much rather see you stick to what you do know—that I am your refuge and your strength, your source of help when trouble comes. Fear can't trap you when you're sure of Me. Let the mountains fall! Let the ocean rage! Let the hills shake, rattle, and roll! I'm bigger than they are, and I'm in charge of protecting you. Tune out the fear pushers and hear this: I'm your Dad and I can handle it!

Your Refuge,
>God

YOU ARE FREE!

**Christ has set us free to live a free life. So take your stand!
Never again let anyone put a harness of slavery on you.**

Galatians 5:1 | THE MESSAGE

My Child,

>Jesus paid with His blood to give you spiritual freedom. He blazed a trail from chains to liberty. He paid the ultimate price to cut you loose from the "shoulds" and "oughts" of the religious police.

Here's how to *live* free: Know that I am real. You don't have to hope I'm real or pretend I'm real. I am real!

Get to know Me. How? Prayer is a great way, and so is Bible reading. Don't make those things into hard-and-fast rules. I won't love you one bit more because you pray or read the Bible a certain amount of time each day, but it will help you to know Me better. That will be the payoff.

Love everyone—even those who don't understand the free life. And finally, don't let anyone put you into a spiritual straight jacket. You are free!

Your Emancipator,
>God

== == ==   == == == == == == == == ==

YOUR SAFE ROOM AND SHADE TREE

He who dwells in the shelter of the Most High will abide
in the shadow of the Almighty. I will say to the LORD,
"My refuge and my fortress, my God, in whom I trust!"

Psalm   91:1-2 NASB

Dear Child,

>If a tornado were swirling across the land, heading straight for your
hometown, you'd probably find some safe, secure room to hide in
until the deadly winds had passed. If you found yourself in a desert in
the middle of a blinding heat wave, you'd probably be thankful to find
a shade tree to sit under.

I want you to understand this about Me: I am your strong, secure
room in the rough winds of life. I am your shade tree in the blistering
heat of your most difficult day. I am your refuge, your shelter, and
your safe place—no matter what's going on. I am a blanket of safety
and a covering of confidence. I am the One you can trust. Open your
eyes to My reality and your heart to My love. I am here for you.

Your Mighty Fortress,
>God

== == == == == == == == == == == ==

GIVE ME A "G"! GIVE ME AN "O"!

Let us consider how we may spur one another on toward love and good deeds.

Hebrews 10:24

My Child,

>Why do teams have cheerleaders? The cheerleaders are supposed to get the crowds to cheer. When the players get discouraged, they hear the crowds yelling and think, *We can still win this thing. All these people are pulling for us.* Why do boxers have trainers in their corners? So that in between rounds, when the boxer limps back to his corner tired and discouraged, the trainer can yell, "Keep your hands up! Hit him in the ribs! Stay on your toes! You're the champ!"

Encouragement can mean the difference between winning and losing, so encourage your friends to keep doing the right thing. Maybe an appreciative note or a Bible verse will encourage them. Maybe telling them how great they are will build them up. Maybe just listening will make the difference. Whatever it takes, do it. Later, when you're discouraged, I hope your friends will encourage you.

Your Encourager,
>God

== == ==   == == == == == == == == ==

SMALL FAITH EQUALS BIG RESULTS

Who despises the day of small things?

| Zechariah | 4:10 |

Dear Child,

>It's easy to look at powerful people in the Bible and say, "I could never be a Moses, a David, or a Mary." Let Me tell you something that might surprise you. Each of them had only one thing going for them in the beginning—faith.

Moses told Me he couldn't speak well enough to confront Pharaoh for Me. I said, "Trust Me, Moses." He did, and he set My people free. David was just a kid with a slingshot who went out against a raging giant. David believed I was with him, though, and he brought Goliath down. Mary was just a teenage girl, but because she believed the words of an angel, she became the mother of Jesus.

My mightiest accomplishments began on a day of small beginnings. My most powerful people are those who give Me faith the size of a mustard seed.

The One Who Works with Small Things,
>God

== == ==   == == == == == == == == ==

I'VE GOT A PRESENT FOR YOU

**You will fill me with joy in your presence,
with eternal pleasures at your right hand.**

| Psalm | 16:11 |

My Child,

>What gives you pleasure? For some, it's a close Superbowl game
that goes down to the wire. For others, it's a quiet walk in the park
enjoying the spring flowers, or buying the new live CD of their
favorite band.

The pleasures of life make you glad to be alive. Now think about
eternal pleasures—pleasures that last forever. Many of the world's
pleasures get old after just a little while, like a week-old Christmas
toy that's no longer any fun. The pleasures I give, however, never
wear out.

Are you interested? Then take some time and get to know Me.
The people who know Me are the ones who discover My
everlasting pleasures.

Your Gift-Giver,
>God

== == ==   == == == == == == == == ==

DON'T FORGET WHO STARTED IT ALL

Who has measured the waters in the hollow of his hand, or with the breadth of his hand marked off the heavens? Who has held the dust of the earth in a basket, or weighed the mountains on the scales and the hills in a balance?

Isaiah 40:12

My Child,

>I take pride in much of the progress people have made. I see the beautiful skyscrapers, the highways, and bridges. I see the medical discoveries that bring healing to people who suffer. I see the amazing advancements in the fields of technology and communication.

I also see the proud hearts of people. They forget that none of these achievements would have been possible had I not created a world of natural resources. None of this could have been done apart from My gifts of human intelligence and reason. People make gods out of money or progress or their own abilities, forgetting to turn to the One who was here from the beginning and brought the whole earth into being. Don't be like those who forget. Remember Me.

Your Creator,
>God

== == ==   == == == == == == == == ==

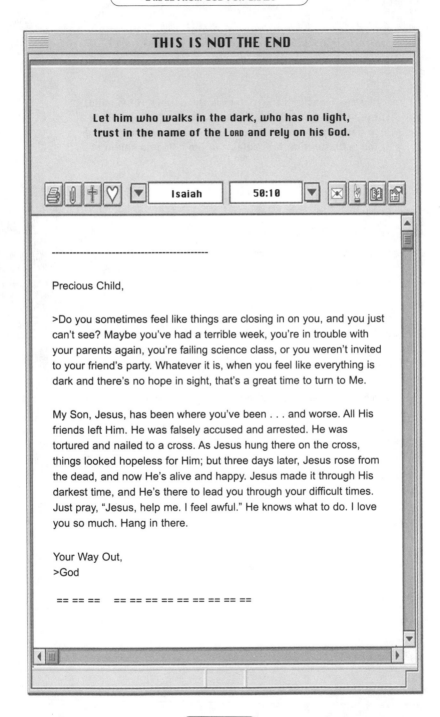

THIS IS NOT THE END

**Let him who walks in the dark, who has no light,
trust in the name of the LORD and rely on his God.**

Isaiah 50:10

Precious Child,

>Do you sometimes feel like things are closing in on you, and you just
can't see? Maybe you've had a terrible week, you're in trouble with
your parents again, you're failing science class, or you weren't invited
to your friend's party. Whatever it is, when you feel like everything is
dark and there's no hope in sight, that's a great time to turn to Me.

My Son, Jesus, has been where you've been . . . and worse. All His
friends left Him. He was falsely accused and arrested. He was
tortured and nailed to a cross. As Jesus hung there on the cross,
things looked hopeless for Him; but three days later, Jesus rose from
the dead, and now He's alive and happy. Jesus made it through His
darkest time, and He's there to lead you through your difficult times.
Just pray, "Jesus, help me. I feel awful." He knows what to do. I love
you so much. Hang in there.

Your Way Out,
>God

== == ==   == == == == == == == == ==

SECRET FOR SUCCESS

In everything you do, put God first, and he will direct you and crown your efforts with success.

Proverbs   3:6 TLB

Dear Child,

>Want to know a secret for success that works for every profession, from the business person to the ballerina, or the taxi driver to the tax attorney? It also works for students! What's the secret? Put Me first

Putting Me first works for every person because I made every person. I gave each of you gifts and abilities. I suited each one of you for a certain work, and when you turn to Me, I can guide you to success. Sometimes I'll do that by showing you how to work more efficiently or study harder. Sometimes I'll do it by teaching you to get along with a certain teacher, coach, or boss you might not like. Sometimes putting Me first will simply unlock for you the freedom of trusting or the joy of learning. Put Me first. You'll see.

Your Secret for Success,
>God

== == ==   == == == == == == == == ==

GO FOR IT, ALL THE TIME

Sow your seed in the morning, and at evening let not your hands be idle, for you do not know which will succeed, whether this or that, or whether both will do equally well.

Ecclesiastes **11:6**

Dear Child,

>It's hard to tell what's important and what's not. You might think that teaching a Sunday school class is so important that you cancel a lunch date with your friend so that you can stay home and perfect your lesson. What if eating lunch with your friend that day was more important to me than teaching the perfect Sunday school class?

How can you tell what will matter and what won't? A lot of times, you can't tell; so here's some advice—just do your best all the time. Treat a homeless person with the same respect as you would treat a famous person. Work as hard in a boring class as you would in an exciting class. That way you'll never have to look back and say, "If only I had known, I would have tried harder."

Your Wisdom,
>God

== == ==   == == == == == == == == ==

YOU WERE MADE TO LOVE ME

The Spirit of God whets our appetite by giving us
a taste of what's ahead. He puts a little of heaven
in our hearts so that we'll never settle for less.

2 Corinthians   5:5 THE MESSAGE

Dear Child,

>Sometimes you feel a deep sadness inside that you may not be able
to understand or explain. Everyone feels that way sometimes. It's a
longing for Me. You were created for fellowship with Me, and nothing
will fully satisfy that emptiness inside but My friendship.

You'll have many other friends in your lifetime. That's good. I want
you to enjoy them, but you need to know that there is a God-shaped
hole in your heart that nothing but My love for you will fill. Here's
something that may surprise you: There is a you-shaped hole in My
heart that nothing but your love for Me will fill. No matter how many
other people love or follow Me, I'll never stop waiting for your love.
You were made for Me.

Your friend,
>God

== == ==   == == == == == == == == ==

I HAVE STAYING POWER

His dominion is an everlasting dominion, and His
kingdom endures from generation to generation.

Daniel | **4:34** NASB

My Child,

>The world you live in is here today and will be gone tomorrow.
Elected officials hold power only from one election to the next.
Investors make a bundle when the market is up and lose it all when
the market falls. Popular movie stars watch their popularity evaporate
when someone cooler comes on the scene. Musicians at the top of
the charts come crashing down when musical trends change.

I've been on top since the beginning, and I'm not going anywhere. My
kingdom has the kind of staying power you'll never find anywhere
else. When you entrust your life to Me, that staying power is yours. I
give you a steady strength—a lasting power—an indestructible joy
that no one can steal from you.

Your Everlasting Lord,
>God

== == ==   == == == == == == == == ==

JUST KEEP READING

**The unfolding of your words gives light;
it gives understanding to the simple.**

Psalm 119:130

Dear Child,

>Not everyone can be a rocket scientist, not everyone can be a philosopher, not everyone can be a great inventor; but everyone can read the Bible. As you read the Bible, it unfolds itself just like a note. When you open a note that your friend has passed to you, first you see a corner of the note, then you see half of the note, and finally you see the whole thing.

If you don't understand everything in the Bible right away, that's okay. Learn from the things you do understand and just keep reading. Gradually, the Bible will unfold itself. A light will switch on in your head. You'll say, "Oh, I get it," and your life will never be the same in that area. You may not be a rocket scientist, but you can be wise. Just keep reading My Book.

Your Wisdom,
>God

== == ==   == == == == == == == == ==

TURN ON THE FAUCET

I will make rivers flow on barren heights, and springs within the valleys. I will turn the desert into pools of water, and the parched ground into springs.

| Isaiah | 41:18 |

My Child,

>Maybe your heart is feeling like a desert today—parched and lifeless. You used to laugh and dream and hope, but not now. Right now, you're stuck in this desert, feeling too depressed to change things on your own. Let Me remind you that you're not on your own. I'm here, and I hear every one of your unspoken prayers.

Here's more good news. Piping living water into dry hearts is one of the things I do best! I can come into a desert heart and cause rivers to flow and springs to bubble up. I can create pools in parched places. You hold in your hands the two faucets that turn on My living water: One is trust and the other is praise. When you trust that I can change things and you praise Me for My mercy, before long, the water begins flowing again!

Your Irrigation Specialist,
>God

== == ==   == == == == == == == == ==

I'M NOT LIKE ANY PERSON YOU KNOW

"My thoughts are not your thoughts, neither are your ways my ways," declares the Lord. "As the heavens are higher than the earth, so are my ways higher than your ways and my thoughts than your thoughts."

Isaiah   55:8-9

Dear Child of Mine,

>Some people who know Me say I'm a "trip." I'm certainly not like any person you know, that's for sure.

I'm infinite, which means I always was here and always will be here. That probably blows your mind, because you're not infinite. You have a beginning. Not Me!

I know everything. I know what every single person on earth is thinking and feeling right now, and I can still pay individual attention to each one. I'm everywhere. There's no place you can go that I won't already be there, even at the bottom of the ocean. I don't have to travel; I'm already there!

If you can't understand what I'm up to right now in your life, that's okay. Trust Me; I know what I'm doing. I have wonderful surprises in store for you.

The Infinite,
>God

== == ==   == == == == == == == == ==

MY PATH IS NARROW, BUT NOT THAT NARROW

**You broaden the path beneath me,
so that my ankles do not turn.**

| Psalm | 18:36 |

My Child,

>Grace is a word you need to understand. Grace is Me giving you
more than you deserve. It's Me cutting you some slack.

Some people feel that obeying Me is like walking across Niagara
Falls on a tightrope. One mistake—one wrong move—and down they
go. They've got it all wrong. I've built you a highway across Niagara
Falls. Sure you'll make mistakes, but you'll never fall out of My grace.
How will you ever learn to walk straight if I shoot you down for every
single mistake you make? Trust Me. I'm not like that.

If you do the wrong thing, just ask for My forgiveness, get up, and try
again. I am for you, not against you.

The Forgiver,
>God

== == ==   == == == == == == == == ==

YOU STILL NEED A SHEPHERD

He tends his flock like a shepherd: He gathers the lambs in his arms and carries them close to his heart; he gently leads those that have young.

| Isaiah | 40:11 |

Dear Child,

>If you live in a city, you may not know much about sheep or shepherds. Let Me fill you in. Sheep are not self-sufficient. If a sheep falls over in a rainstorm, he'll drown because the rain is falling into his mouth and nose, and he doesn't even know how to turn himself back over. That's why a shepherd has to keep a close watch, constantly protecting his sheep from dangers—like taking a wrong path or being attacked by larger animals.

Now I'm not saying you're incompetent. I'm proud of the way you're learning to take care of yourself; but trust Me, you still need a shepherd. You need someone to help you steer clear of the wrong paths and the dangerous situations that can trip you up. I'm here when you need Me. Just ask.

Your Shepherd,
>God

== == ==   == == == == == == == == ==

MEMBERSHIP HAS ITS PRIVILEGES

How great is the love the Father has lavished on us, that we should be called children of God! And that is what we are!

	1 John		3:1		

Dear Child,

>The best title that anyone could have is "child of God." Being a child of God means that the Creator of everything is your Father. Since I am the King of the universe, that makes My children royalty. My children have My favor, protection, and love.

If you are My child, it means you carry My name. I trust you to do things for Me that no one else gets to do. You get to tell people about Me. You get to go on special missions to bring My love into dark places.

Mostly, being My child means you can talk to Me anytime you want, and I'll listen. I'm not a Father who is gone all the time. My main job is raising you. You may become famous, you may even become the president, but your most important title will still be "child of God."

Your Father,
>God

== == ==   == == == == == == == == ==

THAT□S MY JOB DESCRIPTION

You are a God of forgiveness, always ready to pardon, gracious and merciful, slow to become angry, and full of love and mercy; you didn□t abandon them.

| 📖 📎 ✝ ♡ ▼ | Nehemiah | 9:17 TLB | ▼ | ⊠ ✍ 📖 📋 |

My Child,

>I've noticed that sometimes when you feel like you've blown it, you try to avoid Me. You'd much rather keep your distance, because you don't want to face My anger.

There's something I want you to understand. It doesn't matter how bad you've blown it. Forgiving you is part of My job description. I'm a God of forgiveness—that's Who I am. You're My child. My love and mercy are always within reach. When you make a wrong choice and land in a lot of trouble, I'm standing by just waiting to hear you ask for My help and forgiveness. So ask . . . please. You'll see. I won't abandon you.

Your Forgiver,
>God

== == ==   == == == == == == == == ==

NEWS FLASH: YOU'RE NOT THE GREATEST

"Blessed are the meek,
for they will inherit the earth."

Matthew   5:5

Dear Child,

>*Meek* does not mean *weak*. *Meek* means *gentle*. There's a big
difference. A meek person might be stronger than the strongest
wrestler or smarter than the smartest scientist, but a meek person
doesn't use that strength to put other people down.

Proud athletes brag and boast when they win a championship. "I am
the greatest," one famous boxer always used to say. Meek champions
thank their teammates, their coach, and their fans. If you brag about
yourself and hog the spotlight, that's your reward; but if you are meek
and give the glory to others, I will give you a reward far greater than a
trophy or fame. I will give you a place of honor in My kingdom,
because I know you can be trusted.

Your Fan,
>God

== == ==   == == == == == == == == ==

GROW UP!

**Grow in the grace and knowledge of
our Lord and Savior Jesus Christ.**

| 2 Peter | 3:18 |

Dear Child,

>You can grow in so many different ways. You can grow to be taller,
fatter, more obnoxious, or more educated. You can grow in social
maturity or worldly sophistication. You can grow more cynical or silly,
more independent or self-satisfied.

I am asking you to grow in two all-important ways. Grow in the grace
and in the knowledge of your Lord and Savior Jesus Christ. This is
the growth that really changes you. To grow in His grace is to become
a person of compassion, just like Jesus. To grow in your knowledge
of Him is to provide good ground in which your faith can flourish. So
grow up in the things of the Spirit—in His grace and the knowledge
of Him.

The Source of Grace and Knowledge,
>God

DONOT WASTE TIME

Teach us to number our days aright,
that we may gain a heart of wisdom.

| Psalm | 90:12 |

Dear Child,

>"Time is of the essence." I'm sure you've heard that expression before. It just means that time matters.

Do you realize that this is the only today you'll ever have? You can't live in yesterday, and you can't live in tomorrow. You can only live now. With that in mind, don't waste your time. You only have so much of it. It may seem like you will live forever on earth, but you won't; so why waste time on destructive feelings like anger and bitterness? Learn to forgive.

Don't waste time doing unimportant things. Sure, have fun. . . . relax, but don't just sit around. I have wonderful things for you to accomplish and experience, and you won't discover them by sitting in front of the television all day. I have something better for you.

The Creator of Time,
>God

== == ==   == == == == == == == == ==

A KEY TO HAPPINESS

**Give thanks to him and praise his name.
For the Lord is good and his love endures forever.**

| | | | | Psalm | 100:4-5 | | | | |

Dear Child,

>Did you ever wish you had a key to happiness? Guess what? There is one. You might shake your head and say, "No way. This'll never work." But trust Me. My children have been turning this key for a couple of thousand years, and it really does lead to happiness. Ready?

Always thank Me in everything. That's right . . . always . . . in everything. I can just hear you saying, "Surely, He doesn't expect Me to thank Him for the bad stuff." No, I didn't say *for* everything; I said *in* everything. I am a good Father. I am busy working every single thing out for your good—even the bad stuff. The devil is the one causing all the bad stuff. If you will praise Me in the midst of even the bad things that come your way, it will be the key to unlock My blessing. I can turn even the bad things around for your good, so turn the key and give Me praise.

The Lord of the Key,
>God

== == ==   == == == == == == == == ==

IT GETS BETTER, I PROMISE

**Weeping may remain for a night,
but rejoicing comes in the morning.**

Psalm 30:5

Dear Child,

>Unfortunately, sadness is sometimes a part of life on earth. I didn't create the world that way, but when men turned against Me, the world took a turn for the worse.

There will be some times in your life when you are just plain sad. Jesus' friends were sad when He died; but then He came back to life, and they had a party. I work that way a lot. Sometimes things get worse before they really get better.

So when you're sad, just hang in there. In time, your sadness will lift. Even Jesus was sad, but He laughed and smiled a lot more than He cried. There may be some sad parts to the movie of life, but it has a happy ending. I promise.

The Creator of New Life,
>God

== == ==   == == == == == == == == ==

WHAT DO YOU THINK ⌷ENOUGH⌷ IS?

**You shall not covet . . . anything
that belongs to your neighbor.**

Deuteronomy   5:21

My Child,

>Jealousy is an ugly thing. It's one thing to admire someone's new car.
It's another thing to sit up late every night wishing that car were yours.
When you wish you had someone else's stuff, it can lead to stealing.
Even if it doesn't lead to stealing, it always leads to dissatisfaction.

What if you gave your baby sister a great doll that you picked out for
her, and she said, "It's not like the one on television! I want the doll on
television!" How would that make you feel? I'm really disappointed
when you're not satisfied with what I've given you. Don't like your hair
color? Hate your nose? Wish you had someone else's body? I long
for you to be satisfied with your life. I love you the way you are. The
first step to satisfaction is thanking Me for what you have.

Your Loving Father,
>God

== == ==   == == == == == == == == ==

JUST BE YOU

You created my inmost being; you knit me together in my mother's womb. I praise you because I am fearfully and wonderfully made; your works are wonderful, I know that full well.

Psalm | 139:13–14

My Dear Child,

>Sometimes you don't like your looks and you blame Me. You ask, "Why didn't you give me perfect skin like this person" or "a perfect body like that person?"

You're letting magazines and movies define good looks for you. You're listening to the lies of a money-hungry world. They want to sell you skin treatments and diet books, so they convince you something's wrong with you. Remember when Jesus found money changers doing business in the temple? He went ballistic!

You are the temple in which My Spirit wants to make a home, and it infuriates Me to see these money grubbers trying to sell you a lie. I'm the One Who thought you up, and I love what I made! You're the only you I've got, so just be you!

Your Creator,
>God

== == ==   == == == == == == == == ==

FOR YOUR EARS ONLY

**Mary treasured up all these things
and pondered them in her heart.**

| Luke | 2:19 |

My Dear Child,

>Do you know how to keep a secret? Think about Mary. Right after she gave birth to Jesus, all these excited shepherds show up in the middle of the night. "We just saw a ton of angels, and they said your baby was going to save the entire world!" Wow! Wouldn't you want to share that news with your friends?

But Mary didn't tell anybody. She just kept it to herself and thought about it. Way to go, Mary! When you pray, sometimes I will tell you specific things that are just for you. It might be good news about your future. It might be a promise. It might just be Me telling you why I like you. I have secrets that I want to share with only you, but I have to be able to trust you not to blab them to everyone. Can you keep a secret?

Your Best Friend,
>God

== == ==   == == == == == == == == ==

YOUR SPIRIT WILL AGREE WITH MINE

God's Spirit touches our spirits and confirms
who we really are. We know who he is, and
we know who we are: Father and children.

| Romans 8:16 | THE MESSAGE |

Dear Child,

>I communicate through My Spirit. I know that's hard to understand,
but My Spirit is communicating something majorly important to you
right now. My Spirit is telling you Who I am. He's telling you who you
are and Whose you are: I am your Father. You are My child.

It's so important for you to know and believe this. Check it out for
yourself. If you turn down all the other noises in your life—the TV, CD
player, and your computer video games—and get alone with Me,
you'll know what My Spirit is saying: "Your Father loves you! Trust
and believe."

Love,
>God

== == ==   == == == == == == == == ==

TRUST ME, YOU'RE NOT A LOSER!

**Create in me a clean heart, O God, and
renew a steadfast spirit within me.**

| Psalm | 51: 10 NASB |

Dear Child,

>I'm going to ask you a tough question. Are you down on yourself about something? Maybe you despise the way you look. Maybe you made some dumb remark or acted like a moron, and you keep replaying it in your head. Listen, I love your looks, and I'm proud of your mind. Trust Me, you're no loser!

There is something I do want to change about you. I want to change your heart and your spirit. I want to give you a heart so clean and a spirit so new that you'll be able to love yourself as I love you. You won't constantly be on your own case. When you've done something wrong, you'll confess it, accept My forgiveness, and live without this constant self-condemnation.

The One Who Cleans Hearts,
>God

== == ==   == == == == == == == == ==

COME SEE THE LIGHT

Everything was created through him . . . What came into existence was Life, and the Life was Light to live by. The Life-Light blazed out of the darkness; the darkness couldn't put it out.

John 1:3-5   THE MESSAGE

My Child,

>My Son, Jesus, came into your world as Life itself—powerful, dynamic Life—full of energy and hope. He came into your world as Light, blazing out of the darkness, pushing back the shadows.

All of this Life and Light was contained in a human being, so people didn't understand who they were dealing with when they met Him. He looked like an ordinary person, but He was with Me when the world was made. Every single thing in creation was created through Him. No wonder people didn't quite "see the Light" when they met Him.

Although they stood in darkness and didn't understand the Light, they could never put it out! He's still shining! Let Him shine in you.

The Father of Light,
>God

== == ==   == == == == == == == == ==

ALWAYS HAVE BEEN AND ALWAYS WILL BE

The LORD, is the Rock eternal.

| Isaiah | 26:4 |

My Child,

>Eternity is a mindblower. One writer described it like this: Imagine every grain of sand in the world in one huge pile. Once every million years, a bird comes and takes a single grain of sand away from the pile. Once that pile of sand is finally gone, the bird has to bring all the sand back in the same way and take it away again a million more times. In all that time, only a fraction of one second of eternity will have passed. I am eternal.

If you put a rough stone into a rushing river, eventually that stone will be polished smooth. If you leave the stone in longer, it will eventually be ground to sand. I am the Rock eternal. I will never grind down. I am as strong and dependable today as I have ever been. I will always be strong and dependable, so depend on Me. I will never let you down.

Your Rock,
>God

== == ==   == == == == == == == == ==

THERE□S NOTHING BETTER

**Because your love is better than life,
my lips will glorify you.**

Psalm 63:3

My Dear Child,

>Life is an amazing thing! Your mind thinks and reasons. Your body uses the food you eat to keep you alive. Your skin feels the breeze on your face. Your eyes see the colors of flowers and paintings. The fact that you even exist is an amazing gift. What if you had never been born? You'd never have gotten to experience this wonderful thing called life.

Now let Me tell you a secret: My love is better than life. Think of your favorite song. My love sounds better. Picture the best-looking person in the world. My love looks better. My love is more fun than the most exciting vacation. It's more delicious than the tastiest meal. My love is the source of all good things in life. Ask Me to show you My love and prepare for a super life.

Your Life,
>God

== == ==   == == == == == == == == ==

LET LOVE TAKE OVER

There is no room in love for fear. Well-formed love banishes fear. Since fear is crippling, a fearful life—fear of death, fear of judgement—is one not yet fully formed in love.

| | | | | ▼ | 1 John 4:18 | THE MESSAGE | ▼ | | | | |

My Child,

>Fear is one of the most destructive, paralyzing emotions in the world. It can keep you from fulfilling your dreams—doing the things that will make you the happiest.

Fear hits different people in different ways. Some people fear failure; some fear success. Some fear dying, and others fear living. Some fear the criticism that keeps them from moving forward toward their dreams.

Let Me tell you a secret that will rid your life of fear. A heart that is filled with love has no room for fear. As My love rushes in and takes over, fear has to let go and find another place to hang out. Let Me fill you with My love and watch fear disappear. Love is My specialty!

Love Always,
>God

== == ==   == == == == == == == == ==

HAVE I GOT A PLAN FOR YOU!

"I know the plans I have for you," declares the LORD,
"plans to prosper you and not to harm you, plans to
give you hope and a future."

| Jeremiah | 29: 11 |

My Child,

>Sometimes it seems like everyone, including your friends, your parents, and maybe even yourself, has a plan for you. Well, I have a plan for you, too. I created you with it in mind. It is your destiny—the reason you exist.

We have adventures to go on, you and I. There are new friends for you to meet and new places for you to explore. There will be tough times, but I'll give you strength; and when you're lost, I'll show you the way back home.

So when you need to make a decision, pray first and then listen. You will hear My voice like a whisper inside yourself. Trust Me. I only want to bless you.

Your Trail Guide,
>God

== == ==   == == == == == == == == ==

WHO DO YOU SEE IN THE MIRROR?

"You shall love your neighbor as yourself."

| 🖨 📎 ✝ ♡ ▼ | Mark | 12:31 NASB | ▼ | ✉ ✍ 📖 🏠 |

Dear Child,

>It breaks My heart when you are critical of other people. It breaks My heart every bit as much when you are critical of yourself, putting yourself down for every tiny mistake and hating the person you see in the mirror. I'm asking you to stop criticizing yourself and start loving yourself.

One reason loving yourself is so important is that you'll never learn to love others until you learn to love yourself. If only you could see yourself through My eyes. In My eyes, you are so awesome, so valuable, so full of potential. If you could ever get a glimpse of yourself as I see you, you'd never be able to put yourself down again. You'd actually start believing in yourself and loving yourself, too. Then you can let that love spill over to others.

The One Who Is Love,
>God

== == ==   == == == == == == == == ==

NOT FOR SALE

How priceless is your unfailing love!

| Psalm | 36:7 |

Dear Child,

>Some ancient artifacts and treasures are priceless. No amount of money could buy the pyramids of Egypt. A human life is priceless, which is why I hate slavery. Your parents are priceless. Without them, you wouldn't be here.

You are priceless to Me, and I want My love to be priceless to you. How much would you pay for someone to love and accept you perfectly? How much would you pay for a love that never runs out? How much would you pay to be loved by someone who would always care for you, always watch out for you, and never give up on you, no matter what? My love is priceless, and yet I give it away for free. My love is the most valuable thing in the world. Come get some.

Your Treasure,
>God

== == ==   == == == == == == == == ==

GET INTO THE FIGHT

Fight on for God.

1 Timothy 6:12 TLB

Dear Child,

>Sometimes people give up on life, not because it's too hard, but because it's too easy—not because it's too difficult, but because there's no real challenge worth the risk of fighting.

I want you to be filled with the desire to fight for a higher and greater purpose than yourself. I want you to spend your energy and use your gifts for the greatest good. I want you to know what it's like to stand and fight with Me on the battlefield of faith—to taste the triumph of victory in your life. I don't want you to come to the end of your life and wonder, "Now, what was that all about?" Life is much too valuable. *You* are too valuable.

Hook up with Me, and we'll face our enemies together!

Your Champion,
>God

== == ==   == == == == == == == == ==

GET GOOD AT IT

Do you see a man skilled in his work? He will serve before kings; he will not serve before obscure men.

| Proverbs | 22:29 |

My Child,

>Honestly, I am tired of people who don't know Me producing all the great works of art. There was a time a few hundred years ago when My people created the majority of the great masterpieces. What happened? Why did Christians stop painting, sculpting, inventing, designing, acting, writing poems, and composing music for the world?

I want you to learn a skill and get good at it: plumbing, carpentry, architecture, dog training, cooking, web-site design, dancing, or management. Discover My plan for your life. Develop your gifts. If you are skilled at what you do, people will respect and listen to you. While you have their attention, you can tell them about Me; so find something you enjoy doing, and learn how to do it well.

Your Creator,
>God

== == ==   == == == == == == == == ==

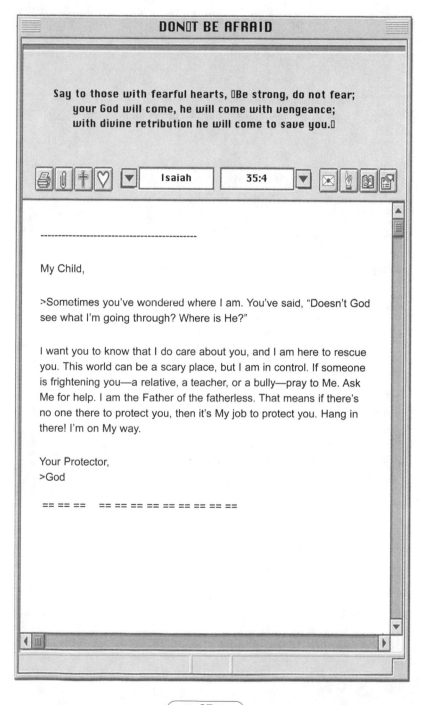

DON□T BE AFRAID

Say to those with fearful hearts, □Be strong, do not fear;
your God will come, he will come with vengeance;
with divine retribution he will come to save you.□

Isaiah | 35:4

My Child,

>Sometimes you've wondered where I am. You've said, "Doesn't God see what I'm going through? Where is He?"

I want you to know that I do care about you, and I am here to rescue you. This world can be a scary place, but I am in control. If someone is frightening you—a relative, a teacher, or a bully—pray to Me. Ask Me for help. I am the Father of the fatherless. That means if there's no one there to protect you, then it's My job to protect you. Hang in there! I'm on My way.

Your Protector,
>God

== == ==   == == == == == == == == ==

DON'T WASTE YOUR YOUTH

Be happy, young man, while you are young, and let your heart give you joy in the days of your youth.

| Ecclesiastes | 11:9 |

My Precious Child,

>Old people have a saying: "Youth is wasted on the young." As you get older, your body begins to fall apart. Many old people can't hike, swim, dance, sing, or even think like they used to. It's a sad old man who looks back on his youth and thinks, *If only I had known then what I know now, I would have done more stuff. But now it's too late.*

Don't be one of those old people who looks back in regret. Take advantage of your youth now. Hike, swim, dance, sing, think, celebrate, enjoy, create, explore, live, be happy, go for it! Don't waste your time worrying and wondering about the future. The future will be here soon enough. Now is the time for you to enjoy your youth. Don't waste it.

Your Maker,
>God

== == ==   == == == == == == == == ==

THINK ABOUT IT

**Within your temple, O God, we
meditate on your unfailing love.**

| Psalm | 48:9 |

Dear Child,

>When was the last time you meditated on My unfailing love? Meditating is just focusing on something and thinking about it for a while. When you spend time with Me, don't forget to listen. After you've talked to Me, after you've waited for Me to talk to you, after you've read the Bible, and after you've read this book, what comes next?

Do this for Me: Right now, just take five minutes to sit still and think about My love. I made everything. I can do anything. I made you. I love you so much that I sacrificed My Son so you and I could be together. I showed Myself to you. Just stop and think about that for a while.

Your Father,
>God

== == ==   == == == == == == == == ==

WHAT ABOUT EVIL?

Yet the LORD longs to be gracious to you;
he rises to show you compassion. For the Lord is
a God of justice. Blessed are all who wait for him!

Isaiah **30:18**

My Child,

>Why is there evil in the world? If I'm so powerful, then why do I let bad things happen? It's like this—I've chosen to let people make their own decisions, and many people have decided to go against Me.

Whenever people set themselves against Me and My goodness, that's evil. I hate evil, and I hate it when people are hurt. The good news is, when people decide to obey Me, to let Me be in control, those people receive My justice.

Has someone done evil to you? I didn't do it. I want to protect you, love you, and bless you. Choose Me, and your life will be better, even though you live in a world full of evil. In the end, I will destroy all evil. Until then, choose My way. I love you so much.

The Lord of Justice,
>God

== == ==   == == == == == == == == ==

BRING THE NOISE

Shout for joy to the LORD, all the earth. Worship the LORD with gladness; come before him with joyful songs.

| Psalm | 100:1 |

My Child,

>People get loud and extreme for rock stars, movie stars, and famous athletes, but they think it's disrespectful to cheer for Me. Do you think the only way to worship Me is with your face in a hymnal, bowing your head, or kneeling? Someone has deceived you.

I want you to get loud for Me. My Word says it's okay. I made you to be the way you are, and I made you part of your generation. True, I made times for kneeling, but I also made times for celebrating.

So if I've done something good for you, if there's anything about Me that you like, then *shout* thanks to Me. If you play music, then write songs for Me, and turn up the volume when you play them. You have My permission to get loud. Crank it up!

The One Who Made Thunder,
>God

== == ==   == == == == == == == == ==

I'LL CATCH YOU

When I said, "My foot is slipping,"
your love, O LORD, supported me.

| Psalm | 94:18 |

Dear Child,

>Have you ever been rock climbing? They hook you to a rope on a pulley, and up you climb. The angle is steep, and the rock is jagged. Sometimes the only thing you have to grab on to is a tiny ledge. Until you can figure out where to grab next, you have to hold yourself there by just your fingertips.

Sometimes your foot slips, you lose your grip, or you reach for a handhold that's not really there. That's when you fall. The good news is that you don't fall far, because the rope catches you, and you can start climbing again. It would be crazy, dangerous, and scary to rock climb without a safety rope, because even the best climbers slip and fall. Life is like the rock, and My love is like your rope. Climb well, do your best, and when you can't hang on anymore, My love will hold you up.

Your Support,
>God

== == ==   == == == == == == == == ==

SUNDAY SHOULD BE FUN

**I rejoiced with those who said to me,
"Let us go to the house of the Lord."**

| 🖨 📎 ✝ ♡ ▼ | Psalm | 122:1 | ▼ | ✉ ✋ 📖 📑 |

My Child,

>Some people see church as a duty. The thinking goes like this: "Church is boring, but if I go, God will like me better." What a load of junk! I already like you as much as I ever will, so why should your church attendance change My feelings for you?

Church is not supposed to be one of those things you grit your teeth and do because it's good for you, like eating your spinach. It's supposed to make you glad. It's supposed to be a place where you can be real about your relationship with Me—a place where My people meet to encourage each other, pray with each other, and celebrate Me. If that's not what church is like for you, then you're going to the wrong church. Come on, find a place to celebrate Me!

Your Source of Joy,
>God

== == ==   == == == == == == == == ==

ACTIONS SPEAK LOUDER THAN WORDS

You yourselves are our letter, written on
our hearts, known and read by everybody.

| 2 Corinthians | 3:2 |

Dear Child,

>Are you more impressed by someone who makes a rousing speech
about world hunger or by someone who gives away money to feed a
hungry family? Are you more impressed by someone who writes a
newspaper article about ending racial discrimination or by someone
who makes a true friend with someone of a different racial or ethnic
background? Don't actions always speak louder than words? They do
to Me.

There are people all around you who may never read the Bible, but
they will read the letter of your life. Hopefully they'll say, "There's just
something about that person that's different. What is it? I want it!" So
write My words on your heart where they can make a difference in
your world.

The Author of Your Life,
>God

== == ==   == == == == == == == == ==

STAY PUT

Remain in my love.

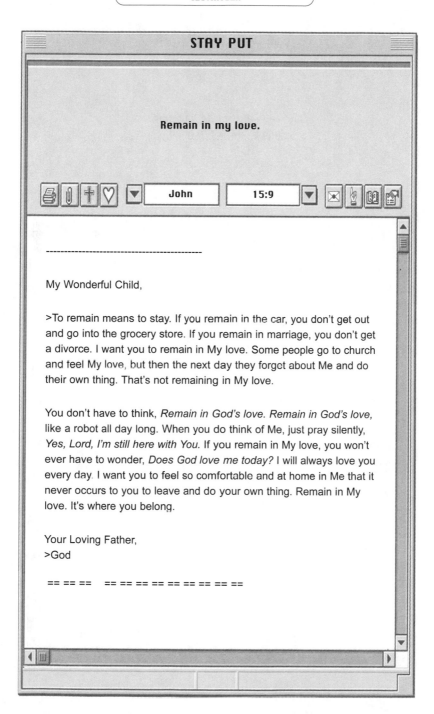

John   15:9

My Wonderful Child,

>To remain means to stay. If you remain in the car, you don't get out and go into the grocery store. If you remain in marriage, you don't get a divorce. I want you to remain in My love. Some people go to church and feel My love, but then the next day they forget about Me and do their own thing. That's not remaining in My love.

You don't have to think, *Remain in God's love. Remain in God's love,* like a robot all day long. When you do think of Me, just pray silently, *Yes, Lord, I'm still here with You.* If you remain in My love, you won't ever have to wonder, *Does God love me today?* I will always love you every day. I want you to feel so comfortable and at home in Me that it never occurs to you to leave and do your own thing. Remain in My love. It's where you belong.

Your Loving Father,
>God

== == ==   == == == == == == == == ==

YOU ARE VERY GOOD

**God saw all that he had made,
and it was very good.**

| | | Genesis | | 1:31 | | | |

Dear Child of Mine,

>When I created this world, I looked around at everything I had made and said, "This is very good!" You are part of what I made, so you are a part of what I call "good." In fact, of all My creation, I'm most proud of you. Why? You were made in My image. You're like Me.

I put a lot of thought, creativity, and love into making you who you are. I have a plan and a purpose for your life. Even when you blow it, I still love you. You can make a mistake, but that doesn't make *you* a mistake. So whenever you fall down, just know that I can pick you up and start you over. You are "very good!"

Your Loving Creator,
>God

== == ==   == == == == == == == == ==

THEY WILL PUT YOU DOWN

Blessed are those who are persecuted because of righteousness, for theirs is the kingdom of heaven.

| Matthew | 5:10 |

Dear Child,

>When you obey and follow Me, eventually you will be persecuted. Persecution isn't only physical abuse. When people put you down for doing the right thing, that's persecution, too. There are lots of people in this world who have chosen to go against Me. When you obey Me, your obedience will bother My enemies, and they will put you down.

When you love people, when you take up for the kids called geeks and losers, when you refuse to smoke or drink just because everyone else is doing it, some people won't like it. When they laugh at you for obeying Me, you are blessed. Why? Because it shows Me that you care more about Me than you do about following the crowd. It shows Me that you are living for Heaven. Good for you. Heaven is waiting for you, and I am proud to call you My child.

Your Proud Father,
>God

== == ==   == == == == == == == == ==

AN ADDED BONUS

That's my parting gift to you. Peace. I don't leave you
the way you're used to being left. . . . So don't be upset.

John 14:27   THE MESSAGE

My Child,

>Most people live with chaos and conflict in their lives: outside
conflicts with other people and situations, and inside conflicts
between different opinions and ideas in their own heads.

Jesus wants to give you peace. When you receive His love, His
peace is an added bonus. When you embrace His friendship, you'll
be able to set Him, like the sun, in the center of your personal solar
system. Then all of the chaotic struggles and conflicts tend to quiet
down. All of the questions untangle themselves. All of the things you
care about line up and revolve around Jesus, like planets pulled into
the orbit of His grace. He will give you peace.

Peace Always,
>God

== == ==   == == == == == == == == ==

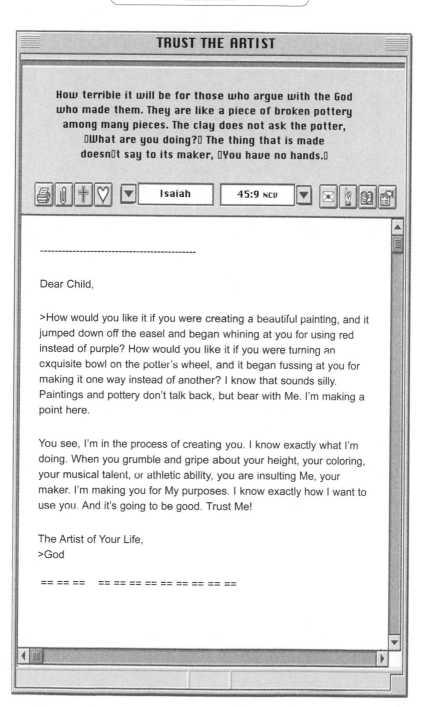

TRUST THE ARTIST

How terrible it will be for those who argue with the God who made them. They are like a piece of broken pottery among many pieces. The clay does not ask the potter, "What are you doing?" The thing that is made doesn't say to its maker, "You have no hands."

Isaiah   45:9 NCV

Dear Child,

>How would you like it if you were creating a beautiful painting, and it jumped down off the easel and began whining at you for using red instead of purple? How would you like it if you were turning an exquisite bowl on the potter's wheel, and it began fussing at you for making it one way instead of another? I know that sounds silly. Paintings and pottery don't talk back, but bear with Me. I'm making a point here.

You see, I'm in the process of creating you. I know exactly what I'm doing. When you grumble and gripe about your height, your coloring, your musical talent, or athletic ability, you are insulting Me, your maker. I'm making you for My purposes. I know exactly how I want to use you. And it's going to be good. Trust Me!

The Artist of Your Life,
>God

== == ==   == == == == == == == == ==

WILL YOU LOVE MY WORLD WITH ME?

**Dear friends, since God so loved us,
we also ought to love one another.**

| 1 John | 4:11 |

Dear Child,

>In the beginning, My world was a little jewel of a planet with fields and forests full of amazing animals, waters full of fascinating fish, and skies full of glorious birds; but My masterpiece was the human family.

My plan for human beings was that they live forever in harmony with each other and Me. They wanted their own way instead of Mine, however, so now there's a lot of sickness and sadness in My once-beautiful world.

Why don't I just wave a magic wand and fix it? Magic wands are not My thing. I work through people like you, who will love the lonely with My love and reach out to the broken with My touch. I need your heart to care, your hands to heal, your feet to go, and your voice to tell the truth. Will you love My world with Me?

Your Creator,
>God

== == ==   == == == == == == == == ==

A CHEERING CROWD

Since we have such a huge crowd of men of faith watching us
from the grandstands, let us strip off anything that slows us
down or holds us back, and especially those sins that wrap
themselves so tightly around our feet and trip us up; and let us
run with patience the particular race that God has set before us.

Hebrews   12:1 TLB

Dear Child,

>Do you realize that up in Heaven, all the great men and women of
faith are cheering for you—Moses and Abraham, Ruth and Sarah,
Peter and Paul, and Jesus Himself? All of them are looking down
from their heavenly grandstand as you run your own race of faith. All
of them are shouting, "Go for it! Don't stop! You can do it!"

What is your race? I have asked you to live out your faith in the
middle of your world—right where you are—in your family, in your
school, on your street. I have asked you to untangle yourself from the
temptations that try to trip you up so that you can step out in love,
reach out in mercy, and take My words of hope to people in despair.
So get in the race and trust Me. You're not running alone. I'm right
here beside you!

Your Coach,
>God

== == ==   == == == == == == == == ==

STAY UNDER THE WATERFALL

Keep yourselves in God's love as you wait for the mercy of our Lord Jesus Christ to bring you to eternal life.

Jude	21

Dear Child,

>If you are a Christian—if you have asked Jesus to be in control of your life—then you are going to Heaven. That's great, but how are you supposed to live until then? Well, from now until the day you die, the most important thing you can do is stay in My love.

My love is like a waterfall. It's always pouring down over you from Heaven. My love will clean you, refresh you, restore you, and feed you. Make sure you stay under the waterfall of My love. That means reading the Bible. It means setting apart some time every day just to listen to Me. It means talking to Me when things are going bad and when things are going good. To stay in My love means to obey Me. Eventually, you'll be here in Heaven with Me. Until then, stay in My love.

Your Constant Love-Giver,
>God

== == ==   == == == == == == == == ==

I KNOW THE WAY

He is like a tree planted by streams of water,
which yields its fruit in season and whose leaf
does not wither. Whatever he does prospers.

Psalm 1:3

Dear Child,

>Living for Me is practical. Think about it. If I made the whole world (which I did), and if I'm perfect and good (which I am), isn't My way going to be the best way?

My methods aren't meant to burden, frustrate, or limit you. I want you to be blessed in everything you do. The Bible is My map of the world. It explains what's out there, and it charts the roads I want you to take. Disregard the world's directions. They will only get you lost.

Let Me lead you every day. I know the way.

Your Guide,
>God

== == ==   == == == == == == == == ==

YOU CAN☐T KNOW IT ALL

As you do not know the path of the wind, or how
the body is formed in a mother☐s womb, so you cannot
understand the work of God, the Maker of all things.

| Ecclesiastes | 11:5 |

My Child,

>You will never totally figure Me out. Don't even try. I've done things
and thought things and been things that would literally blow your
mind. As long as you live on earth, you will only know Me in part, but
that is enough. How can you know Me at all? Because I came down
to your level and showed you who I am.

If someone speaks three different languages, and you only speak one
language, that person will choose your language and use it to speak
to you. Otherwise, how could you understand what's being said?
That's what I did when I sent Jesus to earth. I sent Him speaking the
language of humanity. I sent Him dressed in human flesh and blood
and bones so you could relate to Him. Through Jesus, I brought My
unknowable self into a knowable form that you could understand.
Everything I want you to know about Me you can learn from Jesus. If
you can't learn it from Jesus, you don't need to know it. So get to
know Jesus, and you'll know who I am.

Your Infinite Father,
>God

DONⅡT HOLD BACK!

Love the LORD your God with all your heart and with all your soul and with all your strength.

Deuteronomy 6:5

Dear Child,

>I like Mike. Seriously, Michael Jordan is great. I've never seen him hold back on the court. He always goes 100 percent. Even when his team is winning by forty points, Jordan still plays his best.

I want you to be that way with Me. Love Me with everything you have. Love Me with your body—dance, run, play a musical instrument, skateboard, feed hungry people. Love Me with your emotions—cry, yell, laugh, sing. Love Me with your mind—write poetry, solve difficult problems, draw great pictures. I am passionate! Just look at the intense world I made. I don't do anything halfway. It's all or nothing. You be the same way. Go for it!

Your Full-On Creator,
>God

== == ==   == == == == == == == == ==

I KNOW YOU SO WELL

O Lᴏʀᴅ, you have searched me and you know me.
You know when I sit and when I rise; you perceive
my thoughts from afar. You discern my going out and
my lying down; you are familiar with all my ways.

| Psalm | 139: 1-3 |

Dear Child of Mine,

>Sometimes you feel that no one understands you—that nobody sees when you're happy and nobody cares when you're sad. Your parents may seem too busy. Your teachers have their own problems. Even your friends don't seem to be tuned in to what you're feeling.

But I know. I know you so well! I always have. I understand everything about you—your joy and sorrow. All those thoughts you want to express, but can't—I hear them, because I can listen to your heart. I see, I hear, I care, I understand. Come. Talk to Me today.

Your Loving Father,
>God

== == ==   == == == == == == == == ==

COME LIVE IN MY LOVE

Make yourselves at home in my love. If you keep
my commands, you'll remain intimately at home in
my love. That's what I've done—kept my Father's
commands and made myself at home in his love.

| | | | | | John 15:9-10 | THE MESSAGE | | | | | |

Dear Child,

>My love for you is like the home you've always dreamed about and longed for. Every room is furnished with great stuff—thick rugs, comfortable chairs, and a view from every window. When you walk in the front door, you almost have to stop and stare. There's something so familiar. It's like you've been here before and you're finally home to stay! The reason you get this feeling is that you were created to live in My love full time, enjoying My friendship forever.

How can you pull that off? By living the way I designed you to live. Jesus lived like that. He lived full time within the boundaries of My perfect commands for His life. That's why He was able to live full time within the walls of My perfect love. You can, too.

Your Architect, Builder, and Host,
>God

== == ==   == == == == == == == == ==

DON□T KEEP IT A SECRET

I do not hide your righteousness in my heart;
I speak of your faithfulness and salvation.

Psalm 40:10

My Child,

>One of the best ways to advertise a new product is by word of mouth. If your friends tell you that the new Western Super-Duper Burger is delicious, that means a lot more than any commercial telling you it's really great. Of course the commercial is going to say it's good. They want your money. If your friends say it's good, they're just telling you what they think.

Have I been faithful to you? Have you found comfort in Me? Do you enjoy Me? Has My love meant anything to you? Then tell your friends about Me. They know you. They will believe you before they will a preacher on TV. Tell your friends about the Bible. Tell them about Jesus and the Cross. Loan them this book. Don't keep Me all to yourself. Spread the word.

Your Good News,
>God

== == ==   == == == == == == == == ==

I'LL HELP YOU WALK THE PATH

Enter through the narrow gate. The gate is wide and the road is wide that leads to hell, and many people enter through that gate. But the gate is small and the road is narrow that leads to true life. Only a few people find that road.

| | Matthew | 7: 13-14 NCV | |

My Child,

>Every day you're faced with tough decisions and hard choices. If you're living for Me, it will sometimes feel like you're walking down a narrow road, trying not to slip off and fall into a ditch.

Sometimes you look around and see most people cruising along a huge, eight-lane super-highway with lots of room to maneuver. The big, broad super-highway of life may look easy, but in the end, its drivers will find it doesn't lead to Me.

How do you stay on the narrow road? Get to know Me. Read My Word. Let Me lead you and show you the way. Let Me give you the strength and the balance you need to make the right choices. You can do it!

The Master Planner,
>God

== == ==   == == == == == == == == ==

KEEP IT SIMPLE

Now all has been heard; here is the conclusion of the matter: Fear God and keep his commandments, for this is the whole duty of man.

| Ecclesiastes | 12:13 |

My Child,

>People like to make things more complicated than they really are. Actually, living the Christian life is pretty simple. You only have to do one thing—obey me. That's it. An old song says, "Trust and obey, for there's no other way to be happy in Jesus." Of course My job is a little more complicated. I send you my love, stay up day and night protecting you, make you wise, give you peace, answer your prayers, keep you safe, fill your heart with joy and peace, hang out with you, be your friend, and a million other wonderful things.

But your job is still just one thing—obey me. That's' it. By obeying me, you put yourself in a place to receive all the good things I have for you. Your obedience doesn't earn my love (I already love you), but it sets you up to receive my love. What are my commandments that you have to obey? Love me, and love those around you. Again, pretty simple. If you will obey me today, then you will have done your job for today. Way to go.

Your Priority,
>God

== == == == == == == == == == == ==

DIVE INTO PRAYER

God's Spirit is right alongside helping us along. If we don't know how or what to pray, it doesn't matter. He does our praying in and for us, making prayer out of our wordless sighs.

Romans 8:26   THE MESSAGE

My Child,

>Prayer is an ongoing adventure. Dive into it like you would a deep, clear river and swim! Don't worry about knowing how to pray. My Spirit will be there to keep you afloat. He is the ultimate prayer partner. He prays with you, in you, and for you.

Sometimes you'll have a nagging feeling that there's something you need to pray about, but you can't seem to put your finger on what it is. That's when My Spirit goes into action. He sees what's in your heart—all those things you can't put into words—then He turns your sighs into prayers. Even though you may not know exactly what He's praying through you, I will know—and I will answer.

Your Prayer Partner,
>God

== == ==   == == == == == == == == ==

SATISFACTION GUARANTEED

Then I realized that it is good and proper for a man to eat and drink, and to find satisfaction in his toilsome labor under the sun during the few days of life God has given him □for this is his lot.

Ecclesiastes   5:18

My Child,

>Your job is not supposed to be easy, but it should at least be satisfying. Lots of people think they are supposed to hate their job. That's not true. You won't be satisfied with every single job you have, but you should eventually be satisfied with your career.

If you have been working a job for several years, and every morning you feel like you'd rather be dipped in a vat of boiling oil than spend another day at work, it's probably time to look for another job.

I'm not saying you'll be rich. I'm not saying your job will be easy. I didn't put you on this planet to hate your job. I have something better for you called "job satisfaction." Satisfaction is a gift from me. If you are dissatisfied with your work, pray for satisfaction. I will either make you satisfied or find you another job.

The One Who Satisfies,
>God

== == ==   == == == == == == == == ==

HERE TODAY, GONE TOMORROW

All men are like grass, and all their glory is like the flowers of the field. The grass withers and the flowers fall, because the breath of the LORD blows on them. Surely the people are grass.

| Isaiah | 40:6-7 |

Dear Child,

>Eighty years may seem like a long time to you, but to me it's just the blink of an eye. Compared to eternity, your life on earth is a single breath. I know that sounds depressing, but I'm actually trying to encourage you. If you've made me your Lord, you're going to spend eternity with me in paradise, so what have you got to lose on earth?

With that in mind, don't waste your life trying to impress people or be famous. Can a blade of grass be famous? Does anybody remember a blade of grass? Instead, take chances. Obey me. Tell people about me. Risk embarrassment. Be a fool for me. What have you got to lose? Spend your life following me, and when you get to heaven, you'll be glad you did.

Your Eternal Father,
>God

== == ==   == == == == == == == == ==

I LOVE CRACKPOTS, TOO!

We have this treasure in jars of clay to show that this all-surpassing power is from God and not from us.

2 Corinthians   4:7

My Child,

>Once you believe in Me, I come to live My life in you. One of My favorite things is getting to live in lots of different kinds of people. Then the world sees Me in an amazing variety of human packages: large, small, young, old, tall, short, educated, and uneducated. It's like pouring out a rich, delicious liquid into an assortment of different containers: clay pots, china coffee cups, plastic glasses, crystal pitchers, and pottery mugs. They are all filled with the same stuff—My Spirit—but each one is unique.

Some of My containers even have a few holes and cracks, but I love My crackpots, too! They allow My Spirit to leak out on all the people around them! Let Me fill you up to overflowing.

Your Source and Supply,
>God

== == ==   == == == == == == == == ==

LET ME LEAD YOU

Behold, I am coming soon! My reward is with me, and I will give to everyone according to what he has done.

| | | | | ▼ | Revelation | | 22:12 | | ▼ | | | | |

Dear Child,

>Being a Christian is much more than just believing in me and going to Heaven. It means letting me lead you on earth. Some Christians sit back and say, "Well, I'm saved. I've got that taken care of. Now it's time for me to go make a life for myself." They build their careers without ever asking me what I want them to do. They make decisions based on what will make them the most money, without ever praying and asking me what my will is.

When Jesus returns, what reward will those people have? If Jesus is their God, then they will go to heaven, be forgiven, and all those wonderful things. Jesus is returning with a special reward for those who regularly obeyed me and followed me, however. I have exciting things for you to do on earth, and exciting rewards for you in Heaven. Will you let me rule your whole life?

Your Reward,
>God

== == ==   == == == == == == == == ==

HEAVEN IS WELL WORTH IT

[Moses] regarded disgrace for the sake of Christ as of greater value than the treasures of Egypt, because he was looking ahead to his reward.

| | Hebrews | 11:26 | | |

Dear Child,

>Moses had it all—money, authority, comfort, culture, excitement. Egypt was the most luxurious, modern country on earth, and Moses was living in the palace of its King. Moses left all that to live in the desert, to be persecuted by the Egyptians, and to risk his life leading a massive slave rebellion. Why? Because Moses understood about Heaven.

Moses knew that if he obeyed Me, he would spend eternity in a Kingdom much greater than Egypt. Compared to Heaven, Egypt was just some old, run-down trailer park. Moses' Heaven is your Heaven too, if you'll follow Me. I'm not promising that you won't suffer. Moses suffered a lot. In the end, it will be well worth it. Everybody up here says so.

The King of Heaven,
>God

== == ==   == == == == == == == == ==

FRIENDSHIP IS A TWO-WAY STREET

**I say: My purpose will stand, and I will do all
that I please. . . . What I have said, that will
I bring about; what I have planned, that will I do.**

🖨 📎 ✝ ♡ ▼ **Isaiah**   **46:10-11** ▼ 📧 ✋ 📖 📝

Dear Child,

>Do you realize that I've existed forever, and I will always exist? I'm not just some illusion that you've dreamed up. I really do exist. Even when you turn on the television set or party with your friends, I'm still with you. You just can't hear Me then, because you're not paying any attention to Me.

I want you to get to know Me, but if you don't spend time with Me, how will you know My voice? Friendship is a two-way street. I love you and will always love you, but if you don't spend time with Me, how can you think of Me as a friend? I want to spend time with you, but it's your choice. I choose to love you whatever you do.

Your Father,
>God

== == ==   == == == == == == == == ==

STOP, DROP, AND ROLL?

When you walk through the fire, you will not be burned; the flames will not set you ablaze. For I am the LORD, your God, the Holy One of Israel, your Savior.

| Isaiah | 43:2-3 |

Dear Child,

>One time, three guys—Shadrach, Meshach, and Abednego—were thrown into a fiery furnace. The king wanted to burn them up because they wouldn't bow down and worship him. The fire was supposed to turn them into toast, but it didn't. In fact, their clothes didn't even smell like smoke when they walked out! They were My children, and I protected them.

Now if I can protect three guys thrown into a roaring fire, just think what I can do for you! Are people making fun of you for talking about My Son or Me? Is there some area of your life where you feel vulnerable and unprotected? Are your emotions burning out of control? Pray and ask Me to deliver you from the fire. I will do it. Just watch and see.

Your Deliverer,
>God

== == ==   == == == == == == == == ==

YOU CAN MAKE A DIFFERENCE

Be careful how you walk, not as unwise men, but as wise, making the most of your time, because the days are evil.

Ephesians   5:15-16 NASB

Dear Child,

>I could have mapped out a life for you with no hard choices and no dead ends. I could have locked you into life like a plane on automatic pilot and delivered you from the day of your birth to Heaven's front door with no possible pitfalls.

Instead, I have given you a life with lots of options, choices, and chances; and what's more, I have set you down in the midst of a generation that is difficult and desperate. Kids your age are faced with more life-threatening problems and temptations than ever before. Why did I put so much responsibility in your hands? I believe you can handle it. I believe that with My Son beside you and My Spirit within you, you can make a difference in your world. Trust Me! Step out! Make the most of every opportunity.

The One Who Believes in You,
>God

== == ==   == == == == == == == == ==

I'VE GOT YOU COVERED

Know also that wisdom is sweet to your soul;
if you find it, there is a future hope for you,
and your hope will not be cut off.

Proverbs	24:14

Dear Child,

>Ever since you were a little kid, you've probably heard people ask you, "What do you want to be when you grow up?" You've probably changed your mind lots of times. One year you wanted to be a doctor, the next year an actor or a politician. Now that you're graduating, there's suddenly a lot of pressure to pick a major and to choose a serious direction for your life.

Listen. Don't get stressed. I know the gifts I've given you. I know what great things you can achieve. That's why the most important thing you can do right now is to come to Me for wisdom. Let Me teach you how to hear My voice and how to follow Me. With My wisdom leading the way, you'll find the future direction that will bring you satisfaction and success. Stay close to Me.

Trust Me. I've got you covered.

Your Career Counselor,
>God

== == ==   == == == == == == == == ==

IT🖵S MY WORLD

Every animal of the forest is mine, and the cattle on a thousand hills. I know every bird in the mountains, and the creatures of the field are mine . . . the world is mine, and all that is in it.

Psalm　　50:10-12

My Child,

>The earth is Mine, and I created everything in it. I personally made every single atom in the universe! I own everything—even the things you think you own.

The reason I ask you to give your time and money to Me is that it proves to both of us that you love Me more than you love what I can give you. I know what your priorities are by how you spend your time and money. Do you know what comes first in your life?

The good news for you is that I love you, and I will take care of you. You don't need to worry about going broke. Your Father owns everything!

The Creator,
>God

== == ==　 == == == == == == == == ==

THE BEST GRADUATION GIFT

The word of God is living and active. Sharper than any double-edged sword, it penetrates even to dividing soul and spirit, joints and marrow; it judges the thoughts and attitudes of the heart.

Hebrews   **4:12**

My Child,

>You will probably be getting some graduation gifts to commemorate this special time. Guys usually get five or six shaving kits and girls get more perfume than they can ever use. Those things are okay, but trust Me, most of them will end up on a shelf somewhere in the back of your closet. In a few years you probably won't even know where they are. The gift I'm giving you is forever. It's something you can use every day. It will help you make decisions on tough questions. It will keep you company and give you advice about who to hang out with. It is My Word. My Word speaks living Truth because it's alive. It cuts away all of life's hype because it's razor sharp. If you use My gift every day you'll find out it's the best graduation gift you ever got. Use it! You'll see.

The Word Giver,
>God

== == == == == == == == == == == ==

SAY WHAT?

You shall not misuse the name of the LORD your God, for the LORD will not hold anyone guiltless who misuses his name.

| Deuteronomy | 5:11 |

Dear Child,

>There are lots of ways to misuse My name besides tacking a cuss word onto the end of it. If you say, "God told me to go to the mall," but I never told you that, you just misused My name. If you say, "God doesn't mind if I smoke," but I never told you that, you just misused My name. If you say, "God doesn't really care whether we believe in Jesus, as long as we believe in something," you just misused My name.

There are lots of people on earth misquoting and misrepresenting Me, teaching people that I'm someone other than who I am. To really know who I am, read the Bible. Every word in that book is 100 percent Me. You wouldn't like someone walking around saying things about you that weren't true. I don't like it either. Before you begin to teach someone who I am, find out who I am for yourself. Read My Bible. Get to know the real Me.

The Truth,
>God

== == ==   == == == == == == == == ==

WHO⏹S YOUR FAVORITE STAR?

You shall not make for yourself an idol in the form of anything in heaven above or on the earth beneath or in the waters below. You shall not bow down to them or worship them; for I, the LORD your God, am a jealous God.

▼ **Deuteronomy**   5:8-9 ▼

My Child,

>Have you ever been in a restaurant and seen a statue of Buddha? That is an idol: a man-made image that people worship. You've seen other idols too. Do any of your friends worship rock stars or athletes? There's nothing wrong with respecting or admiring another person, but to cover your room with posters of someone and constantly talk about that person—to be willing to do anything for that person—that's taking things a bit too far.

Is there anything in your life that you think of as an idol? Is there any person, activity, or object that you've placed above Me? Think about it. If you worship your car or your computer, what can mere objects do for you? I am alive, and I want to be involved in your life. Worship Me alone.

Your Creator,
>God

== == ==   == == == == == == == == ==

AN ADVENTURE AND A MYSTERY

I have been crucified with Christ. . . . It is no longer important that I . . . have your good opinion, and I am no longer driven to impress God. Christ lives in me. The life you see me living is not ▯mine,▯ but it is lived by faith in the Son of God.

Galatians 2:20   THE MESSAGE

My Child,

>This is the most powerful mystery of the faith-life: When you trust Jesus as your Savior, you crucify your old self. All of the bad habits, the negative thinking, the low motives, and the gutter thoughts are put to death.

You don't have to impress anybody with who you are, because you are *dead!* Then who is walking around in your skin? It's Jesus in you, making Jesus-choices, thinking Jesus-thoughts, and bringing His life-giving force into everyday situations! Tell that old you that he's a dead duck, and you're living as a Christ-container now. What an adventure!

The Lord in You,
>God

== == ==　　== == == == == == == == ==

IT WAS FOR YOU

It is a trustworthy statement, deserving full acceptance, that Christ Jesus came into the world to save sinners.

			1 Timothy	1:15 NASB		

Dear Child,

>Why did My Son show up on planet earth? Why did He lead the life of a normal Jewish boy—raised by simple parents in a shabby town, taught a trade, trained in a synagogue school? Why did He travel dusty roads speaking to fishermen and tax collectors, farmers and housewives? Why did He silently tolerate a humiliating arrest and a mock trial for something He didn't do? Why did He suffer a painful death on a cross that was reserved for criminals?

It was for sinners. Who are the sinners? Everyone who has ever failed at all. Everyone who has been unable to live a perfect life. In short, everyone. It was for you He lived and died and rose again, so that you would have a way to live as My child. My free gift of salvation is available for the taking. Will you receive Him now?

Your Father,
>God

== == ==   == == == == == == == == ==

THE LOVE PROPELLER

Christ's love compels us.

🖨 📎 ✝ ♡ ▼ | 2 Corinthians | 5:14 | ▼ ☒ ✋ 📖 🗒

Dear Child,

>What drives you? What motivates you? What inspires you? Are you driven to make good grades? Are you driven to be popular? Are you driven to excel in sports? More than any of those things, I want My Son's love to motivate you.

Jesus was propelled by His love for you. He loved you so much that He let evil men torture and crucify Him, just so you could have a relationship with Him. Jesus loves you so much He prays for you all the time. He sends His angels to watch over you. Since Jesus loves you so much, let His love prompt you to tell others about Him. Let His love challenge you to obey Him. Most importantly, let His love encourage you to love Him back. If you are moved by Jesus' love for you, then you will live an amazing life.

Your Motivation,
>God

== == ==   == == == == == == == == ==

AN ADVENTURE OF YOUR OWN

I am convinced that neither death nor life, neither angels nor demons, neither the present nor the future, nor any powers, neither height nor depth, nor anything else in all creation, will be able to separate us from the love of God that is in Christ Jesus our Lord.

| Romans | 8:38-39 |

My Child,

>Do you like adventure movies—the kind where the main character is faced with all kinds of trials and challenges? I love movies like that! There are times in the thick of the adventure when you don't know how things will come out. If you knew, it wouldn't be much of an adventure, would it? Well, you're getting ready to have an adventure of your own. I want you to know, however, that no matter how many challenges you face, there will be one sure and steady force in your life. It will be the power of My love that comes to you through My Son. Nothing can separate you from that love—nothing. That's why I want you to make a strong decision now before your adventure even begins. Decide to keep your eyes on Me. Let Me do the leading. Trust Me to be there. Then let the challenges come— we'll face them together!

The Lord of Your Adventure,
>God

== == ==   == == == == == == == == ==

MIRACLES ARE STILL MY BUSINESS

**You are the God who performs miracles;
you display your power among the peoples.**

| | | Psalm | | 77:14 | | | |

My Child,

>Some people are looking for a big show of power from Me. Some think that if they could just see a miracle or two, they'd jump on the bandwagon and believe in Me. Well, plenty of people saw Jesus perform miracles when He was on earth. Some accepted Him, and some didn't. It's all a matter of what you choose to believe.

You are surrounded by miracles every day. Every time a flower blooms, it's a miracle. Every time a baby takes its first steps, or every time a husband and wife forgive one another, it's a miracle. I still do inexplicable and wonderful things every day—like multiplying food for the hungry and healing the sick. So keep your eyes open and choose to believe. Miracles are still My business!

The Miracle-Maker,
>God

== == ==   == == == == == == == == ==

DON□T LOOK BACK!

Forget the former things; do not dwell on the past. See, I am doing a new thing! Now it springs up; do you not perceive it?

Isaiah   43:18-19

Dear Child,

>Sometimes it's tempting to look back at your past. Maybe when you do, you see a great time when everything was going your way. That probably causes you to long for those "good old days." Maybe you see hardships, a broken heart, and dreams that didn't come true. Those things make you feel sorry for yourself or tempt you to dwell on what might have been. Either way, looking back is no way to live.

I want you to find joy in this moment—to look forward to the exciting challenges that lie ahead. I want you to release your yesterdays and reach out to receive My mercies that are new every morning. Don't stay logjammed in the past. I am doing something new . . . right now . . . this minute. Don't miss a single miracle!

The Father of New Beginnings,
>God

== == ==   == == == == == == == == ==

HEART-TO-HEART TALK

Your Father knows what you need before you ask Him.

| | Matthew | 6:8 NASB | |

Dear Child,

>How would you describe prayer? Is it just telling Me what you need? Would it surprise you to hear Me say that I already know what you need? After all, I made you. I thought you up and put you together.

If there is something missing in your life right now, I know what it is before you even ask Me. In fact, I know before you know. For instance, you may feel uneasy and restless. You think you're just bored, but I may look inside your heart and see that the uneasiness is really a guilty feeling—that you need to apologize to someone but you don't want to face up to it.

Instead of always telling Me what you need, why don't you ask Me to show you exactly what it is? Prayer is the two of us talking it over. Let's have a heart-to-heart talk.

Your Father,
>God

== == ==   == == == == == == == == ==

I□VE ALWAYS LOVED YOU

I have loved you with an everlasting love;
I have drawn you with loving-kindness.

Jeremiah	31:3

My Wonderful Child,

>Did you choose Me, or did I choose you? How did you come to be reading this book? Why is your head full of thoughts about Me? If you are a Christian, how did you get to know Me? If you're not a Christian, why are you so interested in Me?

The answer is simple. Even before you were born, I loved you. Since the day you were born, I have been drawing you to Myself. I have been leading and guiding you your whole life. My love is like a hot, delicious meal. You catch a whiff and follow it to its source. I have chosen you as My child. Go deeper with Me. Let Me love you more. Let Me be even more involved with your life.

Your Creator,
>God

== == ==   == == == == == == == == ==

GO AFTER LOVE

Go after a life of love as if your life
depended on it□because it does.

| 1 Corinthians | 14:1 THE MESSAGE |

My dear Child,

>Lots of people set their sights on some specific goal in life. It's like they circle a dot on the map of life and then point themselves in that direction. They may not meet their goal, but they spend their entire lives trying

Some people may not even be aware that they've set a goal, but they have. One dot on the map says "Rich," one says "Popular," one says "Intelligent," one says "Rebel," or one says "Class Clown." Then every action in their lives is focused on that goal.

Okay, now I want you to circle another dot on the map of your life: "Love." Point yourself in that direction and go for it as if your life depended on it—because it does! Love the people in your life and love Me. That's why you're here. Love is the goal worth going for. Go after love!

Your Loving Guide,
>God

== == ==   == == == == == == == == ==

HAVE I GOT A PLAN FOR YOU!

It is God himself who has made us what we are and given us new lives from Christ Jesus; and long ages ago he planned that we should spend these lives in helping others.

Ephesians   **2:10 TLB**

Dear Child,

>I never just create a person and throw him down in the middle of life and say, "There! Make something of yourself." I have a plan for every life, including yours. You probably didn't look for My plan right away. Most people don't. You might even be in the middle of trying out your own plan right now. Maybe it's not working so well. Maybe you've even fallen flat on your face and discovered what failure feels like. That's okay. Sometimes that's what it takes before a person begins to look for Me.

Know this: Trusting Jesus as your Savior is the first step in discovering My plan for you. That's when you find out how great it feels to do what you were made to do—to use your gifts as you work alongside Me to help others.

The Planner and The Plan,
>God

== == ==   == == == == == == == == ==

GET A LIFE

The Lord is your life.

Deuteronomy 30:20

My Child,

>I've heard people say, "Music is my life," "My boyfriend is my life," or "Computers are my life." When something is your life, that something means everything to you. Without that something, your life is meaningless.

Who will say, "The Lord is my life"? I am the One who made you, and I made you to know Me. I want to hang out with you. I want to tell you things. I want to be your life. A real relationship with Me is the most amazing thing anyone could ever experience, yet so many people die without ever knowing Me. Will you let Me be your life? I guarantee that you won't regret it.

The Full Life,
>God

   == == ==   == == == == == == == == ==

MY ANGEL PROTECTS YOU

The angel of the LORD encamps around those who fear Him, and rescues them.

Psalm   34:7 NASB

Dear Child,

>When you were a little kid, did your mom ever let you put up a blanket like a tent in the backyard? Maybe you ate hot dogs, cookies, and potato chips and read comic books with a flashlight. Everything was cool as long as you and your friend were laughing and talking. When you quieted down, though, the noises of the night closed in on you, and it got pretty scary.

Maybe right now the realities of your life are closing in on you just like those night noises did way back then. I want to reassure you. I am here. Please don't feel afraid. You are Mine. My power encircles and defends you. My angels encamp around you and rescue you. Trust Me.

Your Defense,
>God

== == ==   == == == == == == == == ==

FREE STEAK DINNER

**[The Lord] brought me out into a spacious place;
he rescued me because he delighted in me.**

Psalm | 18:19

My Child,

>Whenever I hear people say, "Oh, I'm doing pretty well under the circumstances," I always want to say, "What are you doing *under* the circumstances? Get out from under there!"

I want your life to be better than just okay. I want it to be awesome! I know everybody has hard days sometimes, but My point is that it will always get better. If you're starving, a peanut butter and jelly sandwich tastes good, but a steak dinner tastes even better. I want to rescue you from your situation. It may take some time, but if you stick with Me, I'll lift you high above the circumstances. I want to bless you.

Your Father of Abundance,
>God

== == ==   == == == == == == == == ==

TUNE IN TO MY PROGRAM

Make sure that you don't get so absorbed and exhausted in taking care of all your day-by-day obligations that you lose track of the time and doze off, oblivious to God. The night is about over, dawn is about to break. Be up and awake to what God is doing!

Romans 13:11-12   THE MESSAGE

Dear Child,

>I realize your life can be exhausting at times. Some days you must feel like you're living in a room full of TV sets, computer programs, and video games all running at once. I know it's tempting to try to concentrate on everything at once, but if you do, your mind can easily become overloaded.

Of all the conflicting screens in that room you call your life, there is only one that contains total, life-changing, now-and-forever truth. That's the screen that contains My program. It's the screen that reveals My heart trying to make contact with yours. So don't get so confused and distracted with other programs that you miss out on Me and Mine. Wake up. Tune in. Log on.

Your Webmaster,
>www.God.heaven

== == ==   == == == == == == == == ==

NOTHING IS IMPOSSIBLE

Jesus replied, ⬚What is impossible with men is possible with God.⬚

| Luke | 18:27 |

Dear Child,

>What kind of person are you? Are you an impossibility person or a possibility person? An impossibility person looks at tough challenges and sees all the reasons they can't be done—all the impossibilities, so to speak. A possibility person looks at those same challenges and sees the possibilities.

The possibility person says, "Sure, it may be impossible if all you've got going for you is your own human strength and resources; but that's not all I've got going for me. I've got God and His strength and resources. All of Heaven is on My side, and everything is possible!" So no matter what your challenge is today, remember that I'm in it with you because I love you. And nothing—absolutely nothing—is impossible with Me.

The Lord of Possibilities,
>God

== == ==   == == == == == == == == ==

THIS IS YOUR LIFE

This day I call heaven and earth as witnesses against you that I have set before you life and death, blessings and curses. Now choose life.

Deuteronomy 30:19

My Child,

>Remember playing a childhood game in which someone would hold out both fists and you had to choose which fist contained the pebble, the token, or the surprise? I want you to know that you're going to be making a lot of choices in the weeks and months ahead of you. You may look at each choice as small or insignificant, but small choices add up. Small wrong choices made again and again can end up moving your life in the wrong direction. This is not a pebble or a token you'll be choosing. The choices you're going to be making are often between right and wrong. Between honesty and dishonesty. Between good and evil. So let me help you make those choices. This is not a game, my child. This is your life.

The Right Choice,
>God

== == ==   == == == == == == == == ==

A SHEPHERD WITH A PLAN

You were lost sheep with no idea who you were or where you were going. Now you're named and kept for good by the Shepherd of your souls.

1 Peter 2:25   THE MESSAGE

Dear Child,

>Picture a rough, dangerous, uncharted road heading up into craggy hills where wild animals live. Now picture yourself as defenseless as a lamb—no weapon, no map, and no guide—unsure of where you are or where you're going.

Not a comforting picture, but a fairly accurate portrait of you before Jesus entered your life. What a different picture He wants to paint of your life if you'll let Him! He knows you, He loves you, and He has a new life for you. He has a road map through those dangerous mountains. He wants to lead you to a place of peace, joy, and happiness with Me.

Jesus is your Shepherd, and He's waiting to lead you. Won't you trust and follow Him?

Your Father,
>God

== == ==   == == == == == == == == ==

LIKE IT SAYS ON THE MONEY

**Do not put your trust in princes,
in mortal men, who cannot save.**

Psalm 146:3

Dear Child,

>Some people are consumed with politics. They believe that once they elect President So-and-So, everything will be better. I don't mind if you get involved in politics, but if you're looking to an elected official to change the world, you are looking in the wrong place.

Don't trust in any man or woman to fix the world. Trust in Me. Governments can pass all the laws they want, but only I can change someone's heart. I change people from the inside out, one at a time. I don't change them with traffic signs and rifles and social programs, I change them with love. So vote for the best candidate and pray for your leaders, but trust in Me. The people who formed the United States government long ago would tell you the same thing. Just take out a dollar bill and read what it says on the back: "IN GOD WE TRUST."

Your King,
>God

== == ==   == == == == == == == == ==

KEEP ON GOING!

By your endurance you will gain your lives.

| Luke | 21:19 NASB |

Dear Child,

>In the 1992 Olympic Games, in the backstretch of the 400-meter race, a British runner named Derek Redmond fell flat on his face. What a heartbreak! In that moment, he knew that all his years of training and his dream of winning the gold medal were lost.

So what did Derek do? Did he sit down and cry? Did he kick and scream and try to blame the other runners? No. As painful as it was, Derek struggled to his feet and began hopping down the track on his one good foot! Derek's dad, Jim Redmond, came bounding out of the stands and put his arms around his son. One step at a time, he helped his son over the finish line.

Derek Redmond acted as I want you to act. He didn't quit. He kept on. Your race won't be an easy one, but I'll be with you through it all.

Your Supporter,
>God

== == ==   == == == == == == == == ==

YOU ARE SALT AND LIGHT

**You are the salt of the earth. . . .
You are the light of the world.**

| Matthew | 5:13-14 |

Dear Child,

>Have you ever tasted food with no seasoning at all? It's blah and tasteless. That's what people taste when they bite into a daily diet of life without My love. My love adds the flavor that makes life spicy and delicious. When you follow Me, you are salt for a bland and flavorless world.

Have you ever walked into a dark room and groped around trying to find the light switch? That's how lots of people feel every day in a world without My light. When you believe in Me, you become a flashlight, shining My light into the darkness so people won't stumble and fall.

You bring light by shining My truth into the hype, half-truths, and outright lies that flourish in this world. Will you be My salt and light?

The Light of the World,
>God

== == ==   == == == == == == == == ==

THERE ARE CLUES ALL AROUND YOU

I☐m single-minded in pursuit of you; don☐t let
me miss the road signs you☐ve posted.

| Psalm 119:10 | THE MESSAGE |

My Child,

>I have posted obvious signs along your path that lead to Me. Keep
your eyes open—there is no way that you're going to miss Me. I want
you to find Me even more than you do. I've made the way clear and
straight for those who are really looking.

There are clues all around you—in the outrageously beautiful world I
made—in the diversity of people I created—in their millions of different
fingerprints and individual faces, voices, and personalities. Best of all, I
planted clues inside of your own heart—a soft voice that tells you with
every beat that I am real, and I love you. Follow the clues.

Your Loving Father,
>God

== == ==   == == == == == == == == ==

KEEP IN STEP WITH ME

Enoch walked with God.

| Genesis | 5:24 |

Dear Child,

>If I could wish one thing for your life, what would it be? That you
would know Me. Not just know about Me, but really know Me.

Enoch was like that. He knew Me. He walked with Me. What do I
mean by that? Enoch learned to keep in step with Me. He knew Me
so well that he could tell when I was ready to speed up and move into
action, and he could tell when I was planning to lie back and chill out
for a while. He gauged the speed of his footsteps by the speed of
Mine. He knew all the ins and outs of the roads I traveled. It was not
a religious, Sunday school kind of knowing. It was an everyday
knowledge of My presence that he experienced in the ordinary
moments of his life.

I want you to walk with Me like Enoch did. Are you ready?

Your Friend,
>God

== == ==   == == == == == == == == ==

LET OTHER PEOPLE KNOW

We have heard with our ears, O God; our fathers have told us what you did in their days, in days long ago.

Psalm 44:1

Dear Child,

>Once you get to know Me, one of the best things you can do is to tell other people how I'm working in your life. Maybe you used to feel depressed, but since you've started to trust Me and read My Word, you have begun to feel hopeful instead. Maybe you used to feel like an outsider, but since you've started to trust Me, you're part of a new group—a group that's excited about what I'm doing. Those are your own personal miracles.

I know that parting the Red Sea was a miracle, but believe Me, parting a sea of depression is awesome, too! I know that creating a world was pretty good, but creating a new group of friends is amazing, too. So tell others about Me. Gossip about the Good News. They need to know Me just like you do.

The Source of Everyday Miracles,
>God

== == ==   == == == == == == == == ==

FINISH STRONG

I have brought you glory on earth by completing the work you gave me to do.

| John | 17:4 |

Dear Child,

>It matters how you start a race, but the most important thing is how you finish it. At the start of a cross-country race, lots of people run ahead, full of fresh energy. Three miles later, though, many of those early leaders are nowhere to be seen. They started strong, but they didn't finish strong.

You be one who finishes strong. Pace yourself. Look at your life and see what it's going to take to finish the best you can. Should you go to college? Should you be a missionary? Whatever you do, don't just do it with the short term in mind. Live your whole life as if you are running a race for Me, because you are. Then at the end of your life, you will be able to join Jesus in saying, "Father, I did what You told me to do. I finished strong."

Your Goal,
>God

== == ==   == == == == == == == == ==

BE CREATIVE

Sing to the LORD a new song; sing to the LORD, all the earth.

Psalm 96:1

My Child,

>Have you ever seen the exact same sunset twice? It has never happened, and it never will. I've got a million of them. I never run out of new creations. I made you in My image, and I want you to be creative like Me.

Say new prayers. Sing new songs. It's great to have prayers and songs that other people have written. They help when you're stuck or you can't think of anything new to pray or sing; but every now and then, get off by yourself and sing Me a new song. It doesn't matter how it sounds. Just sing what's on your heart. It will sound great to Me, and you'll feel better, too. Be creative. I am.

Your Creator,
>God

== == ==   == == == == == == == == ==

DO WHAT PILOTS DO

What is faith? It is the confident assurance that something we want is going to happen. It is the certainty that what we hope for is waiting for us, even though we cannot see it up ahead.

| Hebrews | 11:1 TLB |

Dear Child,

>An airline pilot probably wouldn't get into the cockpit unless there was someone in the tower to help the aircraft arrive safely at its destination. Should bad weather set in, the pilot knows someone in the tower can radio advice on how to proceed through a blinding fog or rain. Should an oncoming aircraft get off track and start heading toward the plane, the pilot may not see it, but the air-traffic controller will pick it up on radar and advise the pilot about what to do. That's why the pilot's faith is in the tower.

If you put your trust in Me, I can guide you through the rough weather of life. That's why I'm asking you to put your faith in Me.

Your Strong Tower,
>God

== == ==   == == == == == == == == ==

DON□T GET STUCK IN YOUR FEAR

Some came and reported to Jehoshaphat, saying, □A great multitude is coming against you from beyond the sea. . . . And Jehoshaphat was afraid and turned his attention to seek the Lᴏʀᴅ.

| 2 Chronicles | 20:2-3 ɴᴀsʙ |

Dear Child,

>What can you learn from a king who lived thousands of years ago? A lot! Jehoshaphat, the king of ancient Judah, understood something I want you to understand. Here's the scene: A messenger rushed into Jehoshaphat's courts shouting the news that the powerful army of Edom was on its way to attack Judah. At first, Jehoshaphat had a natural reaction. He freaked out! It only took him a minute to settle down and look to Me, however. Jehoshaphat knew where to get help, and he didn't waste time.

So what's My point? It's okay to feel afraid. Everybody's scared from time to time, but don't stay scared. Pray right away. I'm waiting here to help you whenever you need Me.

The One Who's on Your Side,
>God

== == ==   == == == == == == == == ==

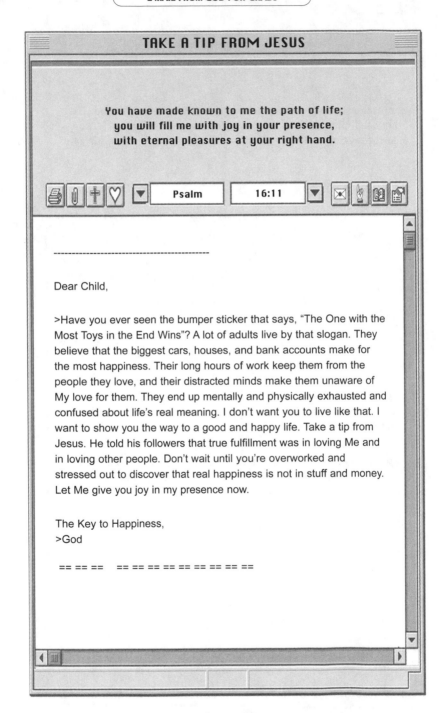

TAKE A TIP FROM JESUS

You have made known to me the path of life;
you will fill me with joy in your presence,
with eternal pleasures at your right hand.

Psalm   **16:11**

Dear Child,

>Have you ever seen the bumper sticker that says, "The One with the Most Toys in the End Wins"? A lot of adults live by that slogan. They believe that the biggest cars, houses, and bank accounts make for the most happiness. Their long hours of work keep them from the people they love, and their distracted minds make them unaware of My love for them. They end up mentally and physically exhausted and confused about life's real meaning. I don't want you to live like that. I want to show you the way to a good and happy life. Take a tip from Jesus. He told his followers that true fulfillment was in loving Me and in loving other people. Don't wait until you're overworked and stressed out to discover that real happiness is not in stuff and money. Let Me give you joy in my presence now.

The Key to Happiness,
>God

== == ==   == == == == == == == == ==

WHAT LOVE IS

Love is patient . . . kind . . . does not envy . . .[or] boast . . .
is not proud . . . not rude . . . not self-seeking . . . not easily
angered, it keeps no record of wrongs. Love does not delight
in evil but rejoices with the truth. It always protects,
always trusts, always hopes, always perseveres.

1 Corinthians   13:4-7

My Child,

>Love is more than a casual feeling. It's more than a physical relationship. It's commitment, honor, and caring.

Love is a runner who never gives up on his race, even though he's exhausted. Love is a soldier who gives his coat to his friend even though he himself is freezing. Love is the poor wife who visits her rich neighbor's fancy home and doesn't think, *I wish this were all mine.* Love is the football star who wins a trophy but doesn't brag about it to his non-athletic friend. Love is the driver who's been waiting in traffic, but lets another car in line ahead of her. Love is the father who can discipline his child with fairness and not anger. Love Is glad when the truth gets told, and it celebrates the good in others.

Love is a song that never ends.

Your Love,
>God

== == ==   == == == == == == == == ==

YOU'RE NO PAPER DOLL

Do not conform any longer to the pattern of this world,
but be transformed by the renewing of your mind.
Then you will be able to test and approve what
God's will is—his good, pleasing and perfect will.

Romans	12:2

Dear Child,

>Some people in this world would like to see you fit like a paper doll in a string of other paper dolls. They would encourage you to clone your thoughts from the tame, safe, unoriginal thoughts of others. If they had their way, your clothes, friends, hobbies, and all your activities would be as much like everybody else's as possible. Maybe you know people who live their lives like that—desperate to fit in with the world's idea of what's important. Maybe you've even tried it yourself.

Well, enough is enough. It's time to stop conforming to the world and start letting Me transform your life and renew your mind. I want to light up your life with original, God-inspired ideas so that you can know My will and step out into the radically exciting future I've got mapped out for you.

The One Who Transforms,
>God

== == ==   == == == == == == == == ==

LEAN ON ME

You brought me out of the womb; you made me trust in you even at my mother's breast.

| Psalm | 22:9 |

My Child,

>Why are human beings born into the world as babies? Why aren't they born fully grown? Colts get up and walk the day they are born, so why are humans born so helpless? One reason is, I want you to understand from the beginning that you are not in control. When you were a newborn, you couldn't feed yourself, you couldn't sit up, and you could barely even see. Without your parents, you would have quickly died.

Now that you aren't a baby anymore, there are lots of things you can do on your own, but I still want you to trust Me. Compared to Me, you are still just a child . . . My child. Rely on Me to supply your needs. When things are too difficult for you, pray and ask for help. You don't have to do it all by yourself. I don't expect you to. You're never too old to depend on Me.

Your Father,
>God

== == ==   == == == == == == == == ==

IT GETS BETTER

Weeping may remain for a night, but rejoicing comes in the morning.

| Psalm | 30:5 |

My Child,

>If anybody tells you, "Christians don't have any problems. It's all just cake and ice cream!" that person is either lying or confused. Sometimes sadness comes into your life. It can even bring you closer to Me. So the next time you're sad, ask Me to help.

Come to Me and let Me comfort you. I still love you, and I won't let you stay sad forever. Life is full of ups and downs, but the most important thing is for you to stay close to Me. If something bad happens to you, it doesn't mean I've stopped loving you. I will never stop loving you. Don't be afraid. I am with you, even in sadness.

Your Comforter,
>God

== == ==   == == == == == == == == ==

MAKE KNOWING ME YOUR GOAL

What is more, I consider everything a loss compared to the surpassing greatness of knowing Christ Jesus my Lord.

Philippians 3:8

My Child,

>It's one thing to know about someone, but it's a different thing to really know that person. For instance, you know about the President of the United States, but if you dropped by the White House today, you probably wouldn't get invited to lunch.

My child, Job, knew about Me, but after he had an encounter with Me, it was a whole different deal. The Apostle Paul's one goal in life was getting to know Jesus. In fact, he considered everything else a big pile of trash compared with that goal.

Maybe, like Job, you've heard about Me all your life. Maybe you can sing "Jesus Loves Me" with the best of them; but that doesn't mean you know Jesus or Me. To know Us is to enter into a relationship with Us. Make that your goal.

Your Friend,
>God

== == ==   == == == == == == == == ==

I'M ON THE LOOKOUT!

The eyes of the Lord range throughout the earth to strengthen those whose hearts are fully committed to him.

| 2 Chronicles | 16:9 |

Dear Child,

>I'm on the lookout for somebody special. I'm on twenty-four-hour alert looking for a certain person I want to bless and strengthen. Who is this mysterious person you may ask? Actually there's nothing mysterious about it.

I'm looking for anyone whose heart is sold out to Me—anyone whose mind wants to think My thoughts, anyone who's trying with every bit of spiritual energy to follow in My footsteps. When I find a person like that, there's nothing I won't do to give that person all the energy that's needed to make and keep a commitment to Me! You don't have to live a perfect life to please Me. It's enough to find a heart that longs for a relationship with Me.

The One Who Searches,
>God

== == ==   == == == == == == == == ==

DON0T FLIP A COIN. PRAY!

Commit your way to the LORD.

Psalm 37:5

Dear Child,

>There are several different ways that your life could turn out. You
could get into computers and write a piece of software that no one's
ever thought of before. You could study acting, music, or art. You
could major in education and become a college professor who affects
hundreds of young lives.

How do you know which way is the right way for your life? You
don't—but I do. As you make decisions in life, pray, "Lord, which way
should I go?" Once you've decided, pray again, "Lord, I believe this is
the way You want me to go. Please guide me. If You want to redirect
me, I'm open to that." Are you facing a major decision like what sport
you should play or which college you should attend? If you ask Me to
help you decide, I will always put you on the right path.

Your Guide,
>God

== == ==   == == == == == == == == ==

I☐M CRAZY ABOUT YOU

We have different gifts, according to the grace given us.

| | | | | ▼ | Romans | 12:6 | ▼ | | | | |

My Child,

>You wouldn't expect an elephant to swing through the trees, would you? You wouldn't expect a monkey to soar like an eagle. You accept my creatures as they are. You appreciate them for what they can do and you don't judge them for what they can't do. Why can't you look at yourself with the same kind of acceptance? I gave you gifts that are uniquely yours. Whatever you do well is a big clue to what I designed you to do. Don't waste time trying to invent yourself. That's not your job. I already did that, and I did a pretty good job of it, if I do say so myself! You see, I'm really crazy about the you I created. Your job is to discover your gifts, your abilities, the things you love to do, and get on about the business of doing them for Me and My kingdom.

Your Creator,
>God

== == ==   == == == == == == == == ==

MY KIND OF PERSON

Jesus called the children to him and said, "Let the little children come to me, and do not hinder them, for the kingdom of God belongs to such as these."

| Luke | 18:16 |

Dear Child,

>Have you ever wondered who I like to hang out with most? You might think it would be kings or presidents—powerful people who call all the shots. Wrong! You might think it would be the most religious people—the ones who could make 100 on a Bible quiz. Wrong again. Maybe you'd guess sports stars or movie stars. No, not really. I'm not impressed with money or fame.

The people I love to spend time with are the ones with childlike hearts—the ones who are not always pushing into the spotlight, but who want to let somebody else shine. I have a heart for the ones who are willing to take a back seat and not act like know-it-alls—the ones who wait for My words and listen for My voice. Are you My kind of person?

Your Loving Father,
>God

== == ==   == == == == == == == == ==

LOVE ME ON PURPOSE

Be very careful to love the LORD your God.

| Joshua | 23:11 |

Dear Child,

>Some things require great care. You wouldn't juggle knives while daydreaming about the show you saw on TV last night. You wouldn't disarm a bomb and casually read a magazine at the same time. Important things require focus and attention.

I am important. As you seek to follow Me, be attentive. Don't just accidentally stumble through your week hoping you'll eventually get around to spending time with Me. Make an appointment with Me. Mark it on your calendar. Set your alarm. When you come to Me in prayer, turn off the TV. Go somewhere without distractions. Be still and listen. I promise that even in the midst of chaos, you will be more at peace.

Your Focus,
>God

== == ==   == == == == == == == == ==

I'VE BEEN CALLING YOU

I took you from the ends of the earth, from its farthest
corners I called you. I said, "You are my servant";
I have chosen you and have not rejected you.

| Isaiah | 41:9 |

Dear Child,

>Maybe you remember the day you first called My name. Maybe you
were in some kind of jam, and you decided it was time to send an
S.O.S. to Heaven. Well, that's not really how it happened. You weren't
the first to call. I've been calling you since I first created you. All
along, I have wanted you to become one of My kids—a member of
My family.

You may not realize it, but you are only reading this book right now
because somewhere in your heart, you heard a still, small voice
urging you to reach out for Me. Over all the competing sounds of CD
players and TV shows, I've been calling. Close to your heart, I've
been whispering, "I love you. I have chosen you. Will you give your
life to Me?" Now that you've heard Me, what's your answer?

The Still, Small Voice,
>God

== == ==   == == == == == == == == ==

YOU WERE DESIGNED TO TRUST

As for me, I trust in You, O Lord, I say,
"You are my God." My times are in Your hands.

Psalm 31:14-15 NASB

My Child,

>Everything is designed to operate by certain principles. Automobiles operate by the principles of internal combustion. Airplanes operate by the principles of aerodynamics. You are a human being, the most complex creation in the world. You were designed to operate by the spiritual principle of trust. You were not designed to carry the weight of the world on your shoulders.

Worry robs you of the peace in which I designed you to live. Worry will only make you sick, so turn your fears and worries over to Me, and I will show you My solutions. You can't control one second of time, how fast a plant grows, or how soon springtime will come; but you can learn to trust the One who controls it all.

The Trustworthy One,
>God

== == ==   == == == == == == == == ==

YOU DON'T HAVE TO PUNCH A BUTTON

Listen to my cry, for I am in desperate need.

Psalm	142:6

Dear Child,

>When you get on the Internet you find all kinds of information at your fingertips. Think how helpful that will be when you're writing a term paper or giving a report in college. Suppose you get homesick. Suppose your best friend acts like a jerk and hurts your feelings. Suppose you feel crushed because you don't get invited to take part in some activity. Will the Internet help you then? No. Nothing takes care of a broken heart or hurt feelings like a friend. I am the best friend you will ever have.

When you need Me, I will be there. You don't even have to punch a button or know My address. I'm always with you. I feel your wounds, I know your needs, and I hear your cries for help. So call My name when you need Me, and I'll be there at the speed of love.

Your Friend and Father,
>God

== == ==   == == == == == == == == ==

JESUS HAS DESIGNS ON YOUR LIFE

It's in Christ that we find out who we are and what we are living for. Long before we first heard of Christ and got our hopes up, he had his eye on us, had designs on us for glorious living.

| Ephesians 1:11 | THE MESSAGE |

My Child,

>When you enroll in college, you take an interest and aptitude test to find out what subject you should study. Those tests can be helpful, but the truth is, you could learn those things (and a whole lot more) just by talking to My Son.

Long before you had even heard of Jesus, He knew all about you. He knew who you would grow up to be. He knew what you'd be most interested in and what you'd be good at. He even had a plan for what part He wanted you to play in life. You can ignore that plan if you want to, but if you do, you'll be missing out on the fun and adventure of discovering your true purpose for living.

Jesus wants to lead you into this adventure. How about it? Are you ready to follow?

Your Guide,
>God

== == ==   == == == == == == == == ==

CELEBRATE YOUR UNIQUENESS

Isn't everything you have and everything you are sheer gifts from God? So what's the point of all this comparing and competing?

1 Corinthians 4:7 THE MESSAGE

Dear Child of Mine,

>There's no bigger waste of time than comparing yourself to others. Someone will always come out looking better than you look, and that will just make you feel jealous; or someone else will come out looking worse, and that will make you feel prideful and superior. Believe Me, you don't need those bad attitudes. They will smother your joy like sand on a fire.

Listen, I made you who you are. You're priceless! I gave you wonderful gifts, and only you can fulfill My plan for you. Just as each snowflake is different, so each person is unique and precious to Me. Just as I created thousands of species of fish and flowers in every color of the rainbow, so I created people of all different colors and races. I love variety! Celebrate who you are!

Your Unique Creator,
>God

== == ==   == == == == == == == == ==

I WANT YOU TO KNOW ME

**The people who know their God will
display strength and take action.**

| | Daniel | 11:32 NASB | |

Dear Child,

>I want you to know Me so well that any doubts you've ever had
about Me will totally evaporate. I want you to have a deep, true,
childlike faith in Me that nothing can shake. That kind of faith can only
be yours when you get in touch with who I really am and what I'm
really like—when you begin to understand that I am on your side, that
I can't wait to take up for you when others are against you, and that I
love you with a love that has no limits.

Knowing all these things, you'll be surprised at your boldness and
ability to take action in situations that once would have intimidated
you. Your boldness will spring not from your own strength, but from
the knowledge that My strength is shielding, sheltering, and covering
you all the time. The key to boldness is knowing Me.

Your Friend and Father,
>God

== == ==   == == == == == == == == ==

LET ME REDECORATE

You deserve honesty from the heart; yes, utter sincerity and truthfulness. Oh, give me this wisdom.

| Psalm | 51:6 TLB |

Dear Child,

>I created you with a private room in your life—a room called your heart—and nobody but you holds the key. Your friends can't get into that private heart-room unless they're invited. Your parents can't either, and though I'm the great God of everything, even I'm not powerful enough to kick down the door and get in unless you want Me there. Oh, I can look in through the windows and see what's hidden inside, but only you can ask Me in.

If I had permission, I would come in and redecorate. I'd strip the gray of hypocrisy from the walls and paint them in the clear, bright colors of sincerity. I'd lay down beautiful woven carpets of honesty, and furnish your heart with graceful, comfortable furniture of wisdom. So turn the key and ask Me in. Then wait till you see your new heart!

Your Decorator,
>God

== == ==   == == == == == == == == ==

FIND YOURSELF IN ME

If your first concern is to look after yourself, you'll never find yourself. But if you forget about yourself and look to me, you'll find both yourself and me.

| | | | | Matthew 10:39 | THE MESSAGE | | | | |

My Child,

>My Kingdom is not always logical, but it is always true. It would seem logical that if you wanted to find yourself you'd go looking for all the things that would make you happy, whether it hurt someone else or not. My way is exactly opposite.

To find yourself, forget about yourself. Take your mind totally off of you and look to Me instead. Care for others more than yourself.

Let Me lead you along all the surprising trails and across the uncharted oceans of My love. Keep your heart tuned into My channel, and you'll be shocked one day to look up and realize that not only have you found Me, but you have found yourself—the one you were created to be!

Your Road Map,
>God

== == ==   == == == == == == == == ==

A PLACE TO REST AND A TREASURE TO SHARE

This is what the LORD says: "Let not the wise man boast of his wisdom or the strong man boast of his strength or the rich man boast of his riches, but let him who boasts boast about this: that he understands and knows me, that I am the LORD, who exercises kindness, justice and righteousness on earth, for in these I delight," declares the LORD.

| 🖨 📎 ✝ ♡ ▼ | Jeremiah | 9:23-24 | ▼ ✉ ✋ 📖 🗒 |

My child,

>As graduation ushers you into a new phase in your life, you'll be starting out as low man on the totem pole. If you're going to college, you'll be a freshman. If you're going to work at some profession, you'll probably be working as an apprentice until you learn the ropes. Being "low man" can make you feel a little like a first grader on the first day of school. You don't have to have a huge I.Q. or excel at some sport or be the richest freshman on campus, though. If you know Me, you know the most important truth anyone can know. If you possess My kindness and My righteousness, you have a secure place to rest and a treasure to share. So meet your new challenges with confidence.

I'll Be with You,
>God

== == ==   == == == == == == == == ==

I WANT IT TO BE YOUR CHOICE

If serving the Lord seems undesirable to you, then choose for yourselves this day whom you will serve.... But as for Me and my household, we will serve the Lord.

| Joshua | 24:15 |

Dear Child,

>Did you ever wonder why I don't use My power to make people do what I want? I could have made the world like a big puppet stage and manipulated everyone by pulling on their strings.

I wanted a real relationship with you. That's why I gave you a free will. I wanted you to have the freedom to choose Me. If I had to force you to love Me, would your love mean as much?

Sometimes you will make the wrong choices, but I'm willing to risk that, because when you finally choose My plans for you, I know it will be your decision. I'll know you have come to Me because you really desire a relationship with Me and that you want this wonderful new life I have for you. That's the day I'll throw a party!

Your Loving Father,
>God

== == ==   == == == == == == == == ==

WORK IS A FACT OF LIFE

Tackle every task that comes along, and if you fear God you can expect his blessing.

| Ecclesiastes | 7:18 TLB |

Dear Child,

>Everyone has to work. That's just a fact of life. It's your attitude that makes an enormous difference in whether you enjoy your work and do it well, or you grumble and slack off. A slacker may not work as hard, but that doesn't make life any easier. It only breeds dissatisfaction.

When enthusiastic, energetic people pitch in to help, they will finish up feeling great about themselves and the work. So before you begin a job—whether it's raking the yard or writing a paper—pray first. Remember that I'm here with you and I care. Work hard and enjoy yourself, knowing that I'll be working right alongside you.

Your Loving Father,
>God

== == ==   == == == == == == == == ==

I'M WAITING TO BE FOUND

"Ask and it will be given to you; seek and you will find; knock and the door will be opened to you. For everyone who asks receives; he who seeks finds; and to him who knocks, the door will be opened."

| Matthew | 7:7-8 |

My Child,

>I've heard you talking about Me with your friends: Is there a God? Isn't there a God? Aren't you getting a little tired of all the talk? Aren't you ready for some truth?

I've got answers for you, if you think you can handle them—not merely intellectual answers, but real, honest-to-God, experience-it-for-yourself answers. Remember when you were a little kid and you used to play hide-and-seek? Maybe you found a great place to hide, but deep inside you were really longing to be found.

Well, I'm like that. I want to be found. So stop all the mental gymnastics, and put your faith in gear. Ask Me. I'll answer. Knock. I'll open the door. Look for Me. I'm waiting to be found.

I Am,
>God

== == ==   == == == == == == == == ==

CLOSE THE GAP

**"Now that you know these things,
you will be blessed if you do them."**

John 13:17

Dear Child,

>There is a huge gap between knowing something and doing it. Just because you have a map of San Francisco doesn't mean you've been there. Just because you've got a recipe for your Great-Aunt Mamie's chicken potpie doesn't mean it'll be on the table for dinner tonight. Just because you know the dimensions of a basketball court and watch it on TV doesn't make you a basketball player.

What really counts is the person who is willing to step out and act on what he knows about Me and My kingdom. Jesus was all action. He didn't just show up on earth one day saying one thing and doing another. Instead, He came to demonstrate what My kind of person is like. I want you to do what Jesus did. Close the gap between what you know and what you do.

The Lord of Action,
>God

== == ==   == == == == == == == == ==

A BLESSING IN DISGUISE?

Do not forget to entertain strangers, for by so doing some people have entertained angels without knowing it.

| Hebrews | 13:2 |

Dear child,

>Picture yourself on your first day of your freshman year of college. You've done your best to fit in with "the look" on your campus—clothes, hair, book bag the whole nine yards. You look like you belong. Then all of a sudden some dorky person—some ultimate geek—walks up, introduces himself, and decides to follow you around all morning. Believe me, I know what you'll want to do. You'll want to find a polite way (or even a not-so-polite way) to ditch him. But hold up. Think about it for a minute. Who do you think sent the dork your way? Could it have been me? Could he be one of my blessings in disguise? An angel? A potential friend? A gift wrapped in funny paper. So give him a chance. Look for Jesus in his smile. I might surprise you.

The Dork Lover,
>God

== == ==   == == == == == == == == ==

TRUE LOVE

Offer yourselves to God, as those who have been brought from death to life; and offer the parts of your body to him as instruments of righteousness.

Romans 6:13

My Child,

>I want all of you—body, soul, and spirit—just like a husband wants all of his wife. When you get married, You and your spouse belong to each other. A good marriage is built on sharing every aspect of yourself.

In the same way, if you want to have a relationship with Me, I'm asking you to give Me your whole self. If your mind says, "I love you, God," but you continue using your body in ways that are displeasing to Me, you will never be happy. If you give your body to Me, I'll bless it and give you physical strength to do the work I've called you to do. I'll use your physical talents, appearance, and athletic ability to help others.

Give Me everything you are, and I will give you all of Me.

Your True Love,
>God

== == ==   == == == == == == == == ==

INVITE JESUS IN

**Here I am! I stand at the door and knock.
If anyone hears my voice and opens the door,
I will come in and eat with him, and he with Me.**

Revelation   3:20

My Child,

>Your heart is like a house where you spend every day. It's where you keep all your hopes and dreams, all your feelings and fears.

Some rooms in your heart hold shiny trophies, but other rooms hide the things you're most ashamed of. Because the lock is on the inside, you're the only one who can invite someone into your heart. My Son, Jesus, is standing outside the door of your heart, knocking. If you invite Him in, I will come in with Him.

Don't worry. We won't be shocked by anything We find. We already know what's in there. We want to help you do some house cleaning, one room at a time. We want to live with you in the house you call your heart, and We will make it a home. Will you open the door? It's up to you.

Your Lord,
>God

== == ==   == == == == == == == == ==

WEAKNESS INTO STRENGTH

**Therefore I am well content with weaknesses, with insults,
with distresses, with persecutions, with difficulties,
for Christ's sake; for when I am weak, then I am strong.**

2 Corinthians   12:10 NASB

My Child,

>Remember the story of the ugly duckling? He was a swan born by accident into a duck family. He grew up feeling sad and incredibly different. It was that very difference that eventually matured him into a beautiful adult swan.

Sometimes the characteristic or weakness that you have hated about yourself can become the very thing that ends up blessing you the most. In our relationship, that's true of all of your weaknesses. That's because your weaknesses make you cry out for My strength. When you do cry out in your weakness, that weakness becomes a blessing rather than a curse. It is the very thing that leads you into my arms.

So glory in your weaknesses. Let them lead you to My strength.

Your Strength,
>God

== == ==　 == == == == == == == == ==

CHOOSE LIFE!

This day . . . I have set before you life
and death, blessings and curses.
Now choose life, so that you . . . may live.

| Deuteronomy | 30:19 |

Dear Child of Mine,

>I want you to choose life. Choosing life means looking at life with hope and love rather than with fear and doubt.

Choosing life means caring about others instead of obsessing about yourself. Choosing life means watching a sunset or encouraging a friend, instead of vegging out in front of the TV set every night. Choosing life means trusting Me to help you do the hard things, instead of giving up before you even try. Choosing life is laughing with children instead of doubting with skeptics. Choosing life is celebrating your own gifts instead of being envious of someone else's.

Choosing life means standing for what's right and true, even if someone thinks you're a geek for doing it. Choosing life is loving Me.

Yours for Life,
>God

== == ==   == == == == == == == == ==

I'LL SHELTER YOU

**He will shield you with his wings!
They will shelter you.**

| | **Psalm** | **91:4** TLB | |

Dear Child,

>Ever get caught in a thunderstorm with rain pelting your face and body and lightning striking all around? Pretty frightening! Maybe you've been in really severe weather, like a hurricane or a tornado. Did you know that I hear from more people during weather like that than at almost any other time?

I love for My children to call out to Me. I love to answer your S.O.S. prayers, because that's one way I can prove to you I'm real. When you're in trouble and you call to Me and I answer, that adds muscle to your faith! So let Me shelter you from all kinds of things, not only bad weather, but from hurt feelings, broken relationships, and tough circumstances. I'll shelter you and shield you with My wings.

Your Protector,
>God

== == ==   == == == == == == == == ==

WE'RE IN THIS TOGETHER

I said, "I do not know how to speak; I am only a child." But the Lord said to me, "Do not say, `I am only a child.' You must go to everyone I send you to and say whatever I command you. Do not be afraid of them, for I am with you and will rescue you," declares the Lord.

Jeremiah **1:6–8**

My Child,

>I know sometimes you feel inferior—like you don't have what it takes to do the things you've got to do. Sometimes you feel like everything is stacked against you and everyone else has more going for them than you do.

Lots of people have those feelings of inadequacy, but you've got a big advantage. You've got Me in your corner! I'm pulling for you. There are exciting, challenging things I want us to do together, and I'm going to be with you every step of the way, making sure you're ready to get the job done.

Don't let yourself get bummed out by other people and what they might think of you. Take their opinions with a grain of salt. I know you and what you can do. We're in this life together.

Your Encourager,
>God

== == ==   == == == == == == == == ==

I BUILT THE CAR

The Lord will fulfill his purpose for me; your love, O Lord, endures forever—do not abandon the works of your hands.

| | | | | | **Psalm** | **138:8** | | | | | |

My Child,

>I have a personal interest in your success. You are My creation—a one-of-a-kind original. I've invested creativity, hope, and energy into making you who you are, and I have no intention of quitting on you now.

You're like a finely tuned race car that I've built. On the day of the race, don't you think I'm going to drive that car to victory? I'm not just going to leave it stalled on the side of the road somewhere. I belong in the driver's seat of your life, so put Me there by believing and trusting Me. I know the loops and curves of the track.

I have a plan for your life, child, and I am deeply committed to the results of your race. Don't worry. I haven't abandoned you, and I never will.

Your Driver,
>God

== == ==   == == == == == == == == ==

SPEND TIME WITH THE ONE WHO IS PEACE

May the Lord of peace himself give you peace at all times and in every way.

| 2 Thessalonians | 3:16 |

Dear Child,

>If you were in the market for great sports equipment, you'd probably look for somebody who knew a lot about sports and sports equipment and was selling it at a reasonable price. Am I right?

Well, if you'd like to have more peace in your life—if you'd like to be less stressed, calmer, and more confident—there is someone I want to put you in touch with. His name is Jesus. He's My Son, and He knows everything there is to know about peace, calmness, and confidence. He's not only the Lord of peace, He is peace. Deciding to make friends with Jesus and spend time with Him is deciding to get rid of a lot of the stress in your life.

As you talk to Jesus and listen to Him, He'll bring more peace into your life than you thought possible. Spend time with the One who *is* peace.

Jesus' Father,
>God

== == ==   == == == == == == == == ==

DON'T BE AFRAID TO SPEAK

You will receive power when the Holy Spirit comes on you; and you will be my witnesses in Jerusalem, and in all Judea and Samaria, and to the ends of the earth.

| | | | | | Acts | | 1:8 | | | | | |

Dear Child,

>Do you feel shy and little bit tongue-tied when you speak about your faith? That's not surprising. When faith is genuine, talking about it taps into some pretty powerful emotions. Never be ashamed of your emotions.

Just pray before you speak, and let my Holy Spirit take over. He'll give you His power and His clarity. He'll help you speak with such simple, honest candor that those who hear your words will be moved by what you say. They'll see something in your life that they'll want in their own. So don't worry about having the perfect words. Trust My Spirit, and speak freely.

The Communicator,
>God

== == ==   == == == == == == == == ==

IT'S AN INSIDE JOB

**The LORD does not look at the things man looks at.
Man looks at the outward appearance,
but the LORD looks at the heart.**

| 1 Samuel | 16:7 |

My Child,

>The world you live in is much more interested in what you look like on the outside than what's on the inside of you. I'm just the opposite. I check out your heart.

I see the scars where you've been wounded by mean words and bad attitudes. I see your hopes—the ones you're afraid to reach for—and the dreams that haven't come true.

If you're willing to let Me move in with you, I'll bring Jesus and all the power of the Holy Spirit with Me. I want to make you stronger and more positive. Believe Me, when We move in, good things will begin to happen. The three of Us work together as a team to heal the hidden part of you. This is an inside job!

Your Healer,
>God

== == ==   == == == == == == == == ==

THE KEY TO LOVE

If I speak in the tongues of men and of angels,
but have not love, I am only a resounding gong or
a clanging cymbal. . . . if I have a faith that can move
mountains, but have not love, I am nothing. If I give all
I possess to the poor . . . but have not love, I gain nothing.

1 Corinthians   13: 1–3

My Child,

>I know you want to do great things with your life. I want that for you, too, but the greatest thing you can do with your life is to love other people and Me.

No matter what you achieve in life, if you have not loved, your life will be a failure. You could be a famous rock star or a powerful politician, but without love, your music would be noise and your speeches would be empty. You could be a multi-millionaire with more money than you could ever spend, but without love, your heart would be bankrupt.

How do you develop that kind of love? Jesus holds the key. Only He can do it. When you let Him into your life, He will love other people through you. Then your life will truly count!

Love Always,
>God

YOU'RE NO DOG!

Do not love sleep or you will grow poor;
stay awake and you will have food to spare.

Proverbs   20:13

My Child,

>How do you feel about work? Do you hate it? Well, you better get used to it, because work will be a part of your life. Everybody works. What about a housewife? Of course she works. What about retired people? They get to work at what they want, but most retired people still work at something.

If all you want to do is lounge around all day, you should have been born a dog. Well, I didn't make you a dog. I made you a person. People work. Even in the garden, Adam and Eve worked. Work isn't a bad thing. It's something I intend for you to do, and you can enjoy it. Do the work I've given you to do. Even if you don't like it, decide to do it anyway. Later, I'll reward you for your faithfulness and give you more exciting work to do.

Your Boss,
>God

== == ==   == == == == == == == == ==

IT'S OKAY TO HAVE DOUBTS

> Then he said to Thomas, "Put your finger here;
> see my hands. Reach out your hand and put it
> into my side. Stop doubting and believe."
> Thomas said to Him, "My Lord and my God!"

John   20:27-28

My Child,

>Jesus is not surprised by your doubts. Even His disciples doubted Him sometimes. After His crucifixion, Jesus shocked them all by showing up in person. To prove Who He was, He let them touch the wounds in His hands where the nails had been driven, and the wound in His side where He had been stabbed. They were convinced.

They couldn't wait to tell Thomas, who hadn't been with them when Jesus appeared. Thomas said, "Sorry, I'm not taking your word for it. I've got to see this for myself." One week later, Jesus showed up again, and the first thing He said was, "Come on over here, Thomas. See for yourself. Touch My wounds." That's all it took. Thomas believed.

So don't feel bad when you have doubts. Jesus wants to help you believe in Him. So do I.

Your Father,
>God

== == ==   == == == == == == == == ==

REAPING THE HARVEST

Do not be deceived: God cannot be mocked. A man reaps what he sows. The one who sows to please his sinful nature, from that nature will reap destruction; the one who sows to please the Spirit, from the Spirit will reap eternal life.

| Galatians | 6:7-8 |

Dear Child,

>You don't have to be raised on a farm to know that if you want to raise corn, you don't plant turnips. Whatever you put into the ground will come out of the ground. That's how it works.

Well, exactly the same principle operates in the spiritual realm. If you plant dishonesty, jealousy, lust, envy, and gossip, the crop you reap will damage and destroy not only you but your loved ones as well. If you purposely set out to plant love, faith, gentleness, encouragement, and grace, however, the yield of your life will amaze you. You will harvest an abundant life that lasts forever.

Your Father,
>God

== == ==   == == == == == == == == ==

SAY THE WELCOMING WORD

It's the word of faith that welcomes God to go to work and set things right for us. . . . Say the welcoming word to God—"Jesus is my Master"—embracing, body and soul. . . . You're not "doing" anything; you're simply calling out to God, trusting him to do it for you. That's salvation.

Romans 10:9 | THE MESSAGE

My Child,

>Some people have a totally wrong idea of what it is to have a relationship with Me. They come at Me with all sorts of accomplishments, trying to impress Me with what good people they are. (If they're so good, why do they need Me?)

Don't they realize I'm already aware of their mistakes? Approaching Me with a false pride is not the way to impress Me. I want to be friends with the person who'll go out on a limb and express faith in Me and My Son . . . the person who'll welcome our work . . . the person who's not too proud to show need.

You don't need to wear a religious mask or put on a big charade. When you tell Jesus you believe in Him and need Him, you can walk right in My front door. It's that simple.

Lord of All,
>God

== == ==   == == == == == == == == ==

LET'S SPEND SOME QUALITY TIME TOGETHER

When he and his followers were alone, Jesus explained everything to them.

Mark   4:34 NCV

Dear Child,

>You are constantly on the move, surrounded by people and involved in activities. How can I get a word in edgewise? There is truth I want to show you, amazing things I want to share, but you'll never hear My voice unless you're willing to slow down and listen—to open the Bible and read.

For three years, the disciples spent part of each day alone with Jesus. He showed them My kingdom through teaching and example. In Him, they saw Me. Though there was a lot they didn't understand, later, the Holy Spirit helped them put the pieces together.

The mystery and miracle of His life is still here for you to discover, and His Spirit is still waiting to help you understand. So pull away from the noise. Be still and listen.

The One Who Speaks,
>God

== == ==   == == == == == == == == ==

YOU ARE MY WORK OF ART

I praise you because I am fearfully and wonderfully made; your works are wonderful, I know that full well.

| 🖨 📎 ✝ ♡ | ▼ | Psalm | 139:14 | ▼ | ✉ 🕯 📖 📋 |

My Child,

>When a great artist paints a masterpiece, he knows it. He steps back, and his heart fills with pride and awe at his work. That's what happened when I created you. I stepped back and marveled at my creation. You are beautiful to me. I made you with care, precision, and pride.

If you are ever tempted to belittle yourself or feel insecure about your shortcomings, just know that you are perfect in my sight. I am totally pleased with my creation. The world is a better place because you are in it.

When I look at you, I see who you have been, who you are, and who I am making you. It's the total you I marvel at. Begin to see yourself through my eyes, and you will marvel too. You are my perfect work in progress.

The Artist,
>God

 == == ==   == == == == == == == == ==

LET LOVE TAKE OVER

There is no room in love for fear. Well-formed love banishes fear. Since fear is crippling, a fearful life—fear of death, fear of judgment— is one not yet fully formed in love.

1 John 4:18 | THE MESSAGE

My Child,

>Fear is one of the most destructive, paralyzing emotions in the world. It can keep you from fulfilling your dreams—doing the things that will make you the happiest.

Fear hits different people in different ways. Some people fear failure; some fear success. Some fear dying, and others fear living. Some fear the criticism that keeps them from moving forward toward their dreams.

Let Me tell you a secret that will rid your life of fear. A heart that is filled with love has no room for fear. As My love rushes in and takes over, fear has to let go and find another place to hang out. So let Me fill you with My love and watch fear disappear. Love is My specialty!

Love Always,
>God

== == ==   == == == == == == == == ==

A RIVER IN THE DESERT?

**I will pour water on the thirsty land,
and streams on the dry ground.**

Isaiah 44:3

Dear Child of Mine,

>Do you ever feel *dry* inside? Do you feel tired of life? Tired of work? School? Friends? Tired of your town? Sounds like you could use a little refreshment!

If I can make an oasis in the middle of a physical desert, then surely I can bring life into your world. The more you open your heart to Me, the more I can send the rain of My Spirit to refresh you.

Cry out to Me right now. Don't hold anything back. Share your needs with Me. Ask Me to refresh you. I want to rain My love down on you. I want to give you hope again. Let Me revive you.

Your Living Water,
>God

== == ==   == == == == == == == == ==

MEMBERSHIP HAS ITS PRIVILEGES

How great is the love the Father has lavished on us, that
we should be called children of God! And that is what we are!

| | 1 John | 3:1 | |

Dear Child,

>The best title that anyone could have is "child of God." Being a child
of God means that the Creator of everything is your Father. Since I
am the King of the universe, that makes My children royalty. My
children have My favor, protection, and love.

If you are My child, it means you carry My name. I trust you to do
things for Me that no one else gets to do. You get to tell people about
Me. You get to go on special missions to bring My love into dark places.

Mostly, being My child means you can talk to Me anytime you want,
and I'll listen. I'm not a Father who is gone all the time. My main job is
raising you. You may become famous, you may even become the
president, but your most important title will still be "child of God."

Your Father,
>God

== == ==   == == == == == == == == ==

CAN I HELP?

**Commit to the Lord whatever you do,
and your plans will succeed.**

| Proverbs | 16:3 |

Dear Child,

>I want to be involved in your life—not just your prayer life or your church life—but your *whole* life. Even if you're just training your dog, writing a story, or decorating your room, every activity goes better with Me.

If what you're doing is not wrong, then bring it to Me and ask for My help. Think about it: I painted every sunset and created all the flowers, so I'm pretty handy at helping to decorate a room. When you commit a project to Me, I'll work with you to make it better. I'm not as interested in the project as I am in our relationship. I love doing things with you. I want to be a part of your whole life. Please share your plans with Me.

Your Creator,
>God

== == ==   == == == == == == == == ==

LEAVE THE DRIVING TO ME

"Anyone who intends to come with me has to let me lead. You're not in the driver's seat; I am. Don't run from suffering; embrace it. Follow me and I'll show you how. Self-help is no help at all. Self-sacrifice is the way . . . to finding . . . your true self."

Matthew 16:24-25   THE MESSAGE

My Dear Child,

>I'm about to give you a hard assignment. Take your hands off of the handlebars. This bicycle (your life) only needs one driver, and I want you to leave it to Me. If you can do that, I promise you the ride of your life!

We will pedal together through surprising and difficult places. You'll sometimes say to Me, "No, Father, this is too scary!" I'll just answer, "Hold on, and trust Me. This is the way." What you're signing up for is not a self-help program. There won't be any New Year's resolutions, turning over a new leaf, or patching up your old self. The real you and I are going on a great adventure, and I'm the only One Who's got the map. So hang on!

Your Guide,
>God

== == ==   == == == == == == == == ==

A REFLECTION OF YOURSELF

**As in water face reflects face,
so the heart of man reflects man.**

| | | | | Proverbs | | 27:19 NASB | | | | | |

Dear Child,

>Looking into the face of another person is like looking into a mirror and seeing your own reflection. You're seeing the potential for good or evil that is in every person. What you choose to do with your potential will determine who you become. When you hate the bad qualities you see in someone else, remember that the potential for those qualities is in you, too. When you admire the good qualities you see in someone else, remember that the potential for those same qualities is also in you.

Let Me help you develop all the good things that are possible in you, so you can become all you were created to be. Most of all, look into the face of My Son, and let Me make you more like Him.

Your Father,
>God

== == ==   == == == == == == == == ==

THE ROCK THAT CRUMBLED INTO A FOUNDATION

The LORD turned and looked straight at Peter.
Then Peter remembered the word the LORD had spoken to him:
"Before the rooster crows today, you will disown me three times."

| Luke | 22:61–62 |

My Child,

>Just because I speak a hard word to you doesn't mean I'm finished with you. Just because you mess up doesn't mean my plans for your life come to a screeching halt.

Peter did the ultimate thing to hurt Me; he denied ever knowing me—not once, but three times. I had spent three very close years with him. He had seen Me heal the sick and raise the dead. He had walked with Me on the water and seen Me transfigured on the mountaintop. He was slated to be a mighty rock for My kingdom; but when pressed upon, this rock crumbled into pieces and lost all hope.

Peter still became the rock on which I built My church. He still became a spiritual powerhouse for Me. He found out what I want you to know. When you fall to pieces, I am the God who can put you back together. I have marvelous plans for your life. When you mess up, let Me pick you up and help you move on.

Your Strength,
>God

== == ==   == == == == == == == == ==

WHAT WILL HAPPEN WHEN THE STORM COMES

Unless the LORD builds the house,
its builders labor in vain.

| Psalm | | 127:1 | |

Dear Child,

>In some parts of the world, where storms are terrible and regular, people build their houses out of bamboo and paper. Every year or so, storms wipe out everything. Because the people realize their houses are just going to get knocked down, they don't waste their time and effort trying to build strong houses. This is smart.

You can't build a strong, successful life all on your own. Apart from Me, you'll work to make your life look good, but something will always come along to knock it down. I am the only One with enough power and wisdom to build a life that will withstand the storms.

So get smart. Forget your own plans. Let Me show you My plans and help you build a strong, successful life. My work lasts.

The Master Architect,
>God

== == ==   == == == == == == == == ==

JESUS KNOWS WHAT YOU'RE GOING THROUGH

We don't have a priest who is out of touch
with our reality. He's been through weakness
and testing, experienced it all—all but the sin.

| Hebrews 4:15 | THE MESSAGE |

Dear Child of Mine,

>You might picture Jesus as wearing a halo and hanging out in Heaven with a bunch of angels. It's true that He lives in Heaven now, but don't ever forget that He was a real flesh-and-blood human being just like you when He lived in Israel.

In fact, He experienced a lot of the same things you do. He felt everything you feel. He laughed and cried. He got homesick. He got hungry, angry, lonely, and tired. He felt hurt and disappointment. He was happy and excited. He celebrated. He struggled and was tired, troubled, and tempted.

He never wants you to forget that whatever you're going through now, He's been there before you, and He wants to help. Jesus understands.

Your Loving Father,
>God

== == ==   == == == == == == == == ==

TAKE ME AT MY WORD

Heal me, O LORD, and I will be healed; save me and I will be saved, for You are my praise.

Jeremiah 17:14 NASB

Dear Child,

>When you begin to take Me at My word, so many things will change in your life. I have said that you are My own creation, and yet at times, you see yourself as less than worthwhile. I have said that I have a plan and a purpose for your life, and yet there are days when you feel hopeless. I have said that I love you and will never leave you, and yet at times, you feel unloved and alone. I have told you not to be afraid, and yet you battle so many fears.

My words contain power, but they cannot help you until you believe them. I am a Guide, a Friend, and a Father, but I cannot touch you unless you let Me near. The way to life is simple and straightforward. Know Me, trust My Word completely, call on Me, and I'll take action in your life.

The Healer,
>God

== == ==   == == == == == == == == ==

IT'S TIME TO GROW UP

**Break up your unplowed ground; for it is
time to seek the LORD, until he comes
and showers righteousness on you.**

		Hosea		10:12			

My Child,

>Before a farmer plants a field, he plows it up. After plowing, the field just looks like a big pile of stirred-up dirt. It looks worse than before it was plowed, but that's the only way the seeds will ever take root.

I want to stir things up for you, too. If everything's perfect in your life right now, and you don't want it to improve, put down this book and stop seeking Me. If you stick with Me, I'm going to change things. I want to plant good things in your life.

Trust Me, you're going to like the improvements I make. My changes will be worth it all. I promise!

Your Father,
>God

== == ==   == == == == == == == == ==

GET SET FREE

"Then you will know the truth,
and the truth will set you free."

| John | 8:32 |

My Child,

>Truth is the most freeing thing in the world. When you know the truth and live your life by it, you don't have to make up any excuses or alibis.

When you live in a truthful way, you aren't saying something to one person and something else to another person and then trying to remember what you said to whom. You can speak your mind and show your feelings without fear. You can simply be yourself and know it's enough.

I want you to know the truth deep inside yourself, so that you don't have to waste your energy untangling a lot of lies, fibs, and half-truths. I want you to experience the freedom that comes with being totally honest. Most of all, I want you to know Jesus. He is the Truth.

Your Father,
>God

== == ==   == == == == == == == == ==

MY UNIQUE PERSPECTIVE

**Do not be wise in your own eyes;
fear the Lord and shun evil.**

| Proverbs | 3:7 |

My Child,

>Are you following your own personal life plan? Have you said things like "I'll marry at this point; I'll have children here; I'll concentrate on my career at this point" and so on? Your plan of action may seem very wise according to your view of things, but it's like the old saying: "You can't see the forest for the trees." You are too close to your own life to have the perspective you need.

I am over you, beside you, and within you, which gives Me a unique perspective. What's more, I'm the one who created you, and I know what's best for you. So don't go with your own program. Trust Me to show you Mine. Then follow it.

The One Who Knows What's Best,
>God

== == ==   == == == == == == == == ==

DO YOU KNOW YOUR JOB?

John [the Baptist] replied, "God in heaven appoints each man's work. My work is to prepare the way for that man [Jesus] so that everyone will go to him."

John 3:27–28 TLB

Dear Child,

>John the Baptist was Jesus' cousin. He dressed in animal skins and ate a weird health-food diet. John was unusual, but people were attracted to listen to him anyway. John was one of a few people who actually knew that Jesus was the Messiah, and he understood how I wanted him to use that knowledge. I used John's gift of honest speech to call people away from their sins and toward their Savior. John's followers tried to make him jealous of Jesus, but he wouldn't go there. He knew that his job was not to be the Savior, but to help others *know* the Savior.

Would it surprise you to know that everybody was created to use their unique gifts to do the same job that John did—to point others to Jesus? Even you! Let Me show you how.

Your Loving Boss,
>God

== == ==   == == == == == == == == ==

I WILL LIFT YOU UP

**Humble yourselves before the Lord,
and he will lift you up.**

| | | | | | James | | 4:10 | | | | | |

My Child,

>Look around you. Who are the people that are the most stressed out and unhappy? Aren't they the ones who are constantly trying to beat out other people? The ones who put down other people to make themselves look good?

Let Me tell you a secret. You can be a winner without putting down anybody. You can pull for others instead of trying to beat them out. Your only competition should be between yourself as you are and yourself as you want to be. In that competition, your own progress will be your prize.

As you learn to always pull for others without pushing yourself to the front, you'll find that I'll lift you up.

Your Father,
>God

== == ==   == == == == == == == == ==

LET ME STRENGTHEN YOUR FAITH

"If you have faith as small as a mustard seed,
you can say to this mountain, 'Move from
here to there' and it will move.
Nothing will be impossible for you."

Matthew **17:20**

My Child,

>I know that sometimes you pray as hard as you know how and things just don't turn out the way you prayed they would. Then you wonder where I was all that time. Did I hear you? Of course I did.

Although you can't see Me, I'm always here. I know life feels unfair at times, but prayer doesn't work like a soda machine where you drop in the change and out pops the can. Prayer works on faith. When you're confused, bring Me the jumbled mix of feelings you have inside, and I'll give you faith.

Faith doesn't take a detour around pain; it builds a road through your pain. Faith doesn't make things easy, but it does give you extra strength for hard times. Faith can move mountains, even mountains like fear, loneliness, and hopelessness. Let Me strengthen your faith.

Your Faithful Friend,
>God

== == ==   == == == == == == == == ==

HOLD ON TO ME

In all these things we overwhelmingly conquer through Him who loved us.

Romans | 8:37 NASB

Dear Child,

>During World War II, a Dutch watchmaker named Corrie ten Boom was imprisoned in the Nazi death camps for helping Jews escape from Holland. There she endured the loss of beloved family members—her father and her sister, Betsie. She was beaten and starved. She was exposed to terrible weather, wearing little clothing, and was cruelly humiliated by the guards. She could echo Paul's words with all her heart: "In all these things we overwhelmingly conquer through Him who loved us."

You probably haven't had an opportunity to test the truth of those words to this degree yet, but I want you to know this. No matter what you go through in your life, if you hold on to Me, you'll find out that those words are true. In My love, you can conquer all things.

Your Ever-Present Father,
>God

== == ==   == == == == == == == == ==

MAKE A ROAD IN YOUR HEART

Prepare a road for the Lord to travel on! Widen the pathway before him! Level the mountains! Fill up the valleys! Straighten the curves! Smooth out the ruts! And then mankind shall see the Savior sent from God.

| Luke | 3:4-6 TLB |

My Child,

>I want you to make a road in your heart which Jesus can travel on. With the help of My Holy Spirit, cut down all the undergrowth of meaningless activities. Level the mountains of self-centeredness and conceit. Fill up the valleys of low self-worth and depression. Straighten out any crooked motives or twisted justifications. Smooth out the ruts of procrastination and laziness.

With a smooth road to travel on, Jesus can move freely through your life, making the kind of difference He longs to make in you. He can lead and guide you, and you will find a new freedom to follow Him. The more you follow Him, the more you will be like Him. Then the people around you will be able to see Him in you!

Your Way-Maker,
>God

== == ==   == == == == == == == == ==

WANT MY OPINION?

He has showed you, O man, what is good.
And what does the Lᴏʀᴅ require of you?
To act justly and to love mercy and
to walk humbly with your God.

| Micah | 6:8 |

Dear Child,

>What's important to you? Some people think money is the name of the game. They keep up with the latest investment schemes so they can score big bucks. Some people think outward appearances are where it's at. They invest everything in trying to look good.

Are you interested in My opinion? Three things really matter to Me: First, I want you to act justly. When you make a promise, keep it. Stand by your beliefs. Second, I want you to love mercy. That means you can't hold grudges. You have to be willing to forgive. Third, I want you to live humbly with Me—not always wanting your own way—but learning to want Mine. It means knowing you are My child.

Your Father,
>God

== == ==   == == == == == == == == ==

THE GOOD, THE BAD, AND THE UGLY

> "First clean the inside of the cup and of the dish,
> so that the outside of it may become clean also."

Matthew **23:26**

My Child,

>Many people spend all their time and energy trying to make a great-looking external person who will be acceptable and pleasing to others and also to Me. The outside is not all that interests Me. I'm interested in everything: the good, the bad, and the ugly.

If you paint a house perfectly on the outside, but leave the inside with rotten wood and no amenities, then the house doesn't bless the people who live there. It only blesses the neighbors and the passers-by. I live inside of you, and *so do you.* You are a temple for My Holy Spirit. It's time to stop doing all the exterior work to make you appear good to others. It's time to start blessing Me by cleaning yourself up on the inside. Appearing holy and being holy are two very different things.

So, let's get started on the inside!

The One Who Lives in You,
>God

YOU'LL THANK ME LATER

**My son, do not make light of the Lord's discipline,
and do not lose heart when he rebukes you,
ecause the Lord disciplines those he loves,
and he punishes everyone he accepts as a son.**

| Hebrews | 12:5-6 |

My Child,

>Think about a marathon runner and his coach. Some days the runner doesn't feel like running, but the coach will motivate the runner to run anyway. The runner might hate his coach during the training period, but on race day, after the victory is won, both runner and coach will rejoice.

I'm your Coach for life. I'll challenge and discipline you in preparation for victory. I have a race for you to run. There are things I want you to accomplish. I value you and your success. I correct you because I love you, and I want you to win. Hang in there and trust Me.

Your Coach,
>God

== == ==   == == == == == == == == ==

YOU'RE ONLY HUMAN

**[The Lord] knows how we are formed,
he remembers that we are dust.**

Psalm 103:14

Dear Child,

>I would make an A+ in biology class because I wrote the book on you. Not only do I know how you function physically, but I understand all of your emotions and thinking processes.

Since I created you, I know you inside out. I know what you can and cannot do. I don't expect you to do the impossible. I know you're going to fail at many things. You're just a person. So don't be so hard on yourself. A lot of times you expect more from yourself than I do.

When I live in you, I'll never fail. The impossible is My job, not yours. Your job is to be My friend. You're doing great, and I'm proud of you. Cut yourself some slack!

Your Creator,
>God

== == ==   == == == == == == == == ==

SPEAK MY TRUTH

Nations are in uproar, kingdoms fall; he lifts his voice, the earth melts. The LORD Almighty is with us; the God of Jacob is our fortress.

| Psalm | 46:6-7 |

Dear Child,

>Do you ever watch the news? If you do, you know what an uproar the world is in most of the time. There are wars scattered all across the globe. People are killing each other for every kind of reason, most of them motivated by greed and a hunger for power. Families are being uprooted and separated. Innocent children are suffering. How I long to be a refuge to those people who will cry out to Me! Lots of them don't even know I exist.

I need you to help bring My truth into this world at war. I need you to speak with My voice so that people will know how close I am and how much I care. In the middle of every kind of conflict, I am waiting for a chance to shelter My people.

The Lord of Hosts,
>God

== == ==   == == == == == == == == ==

NOT YOUR TEACHER BUT YOUR MASTER

I will instruct you and teach you in the way you should go; I will counsel you and watch over you.

| Psalm | 32:8 |

My Child,

>Long ago in Asia, when a young man who wanted to learn a skill, he would become an apprentice to a master rather than attending college. Night and day, the young man would work in the master's shop, watching, helping out, and practicing. The master would not just *tell* him how to work, but he would *show* him.

I want to be your Master. I want to see you more than once a week in Sunday School. I want to live with you, day in and day out. Isn't that how My Son, Jesus, taught His followers? I want you to come to Me every time you need help. Talk to Me and listen. Read in the Bible about the work I've done. Watch Me working in the world. I'm not your professor or your preacher. I am . . .

Your Master,
>God

== == ==   == == == == == == == == ==

I DON'T THINK LIKE YOU DO

How great are his wisdom and knowledge and riches!
How impossible it is for us to understand his decisions and his
methods! For who among us can know the mind of the Lord?
Who knows enough to be his counselor and guide?

| Romans | 11:33-34 TLB |

Dear Child,

>Sometimes you look at what's going on in the world, and you want
to say, "God, what are You up to? This doesn't make sense!" When
that happens, it shouldn't surprise you. You were not designed to
understand everything about Me.

You see, I don't think like you do. In fact, it's actually impossible for
you to get inside My mind and understand My God-thoughts. That's
why it would be a mistake for you to try to figure out everything and
give Me advice. You weren't cut out to be My counselor. The best
thing you can do is to know My character—that I am a good and
faithful Father who will never let you down.

Trust Me in every situation as I lead you, and you'll find yourself living
in more peace than you thought possible.

The Higher One,
>God

== == ==   == == == == == == == == ==

FRESH INGREDIENTS MAKE THE DIFFERENCE

Summing it all up, friends, I'd say you'll do best
filling your minds . . . [with] things true, noble,
reputable, authentic, compelling, gracious—
the best, not the worst; the beautiful, not
the ugly; things to praise, not things to curse.

 Philippians **4:8 THE MESSAGE**

Dear Child,

>Any good cook will tell you that the success of a dish depends on fresh ingredients. Try making a delicious stew out of rancid meat and rotten vegetables. No matter what spices you add or how long you cook it, you're going to end up with a terrible tasting mess.

Instead, when you begin with good, fresh vegetables and fresh, prime meat and add the right combination of spices, you'll want a second helping! The same principle applies to your life. If you fill your head with rotten ingredients, like violence, hatred, and other trash, you're going to cook up a life that's far from delicious.

Use My favorite recipe: Fill your mind with what is true, beautiful, and good; add My love, then enjoy the best life you've ever tasted!

Your Chef,
>God

== == ==   == == == == == == == == ==

THERE AND HERE

This is love: not that we loved God,
but that he loved us.

1 John   4:10

My Child,

>I chose you before you chose Me. I loved you before you ever decided to love Me back. I put a plan in motion for your redemption before you ever thought about your own salvation. Before you felt the pain, My healing was available. Even when you felt as if I was a million miles away, I had My arms around you. In the most painful time in your life, I was there, holding you; and the times when it all fell apart, I was the only one Who could put it back together.

It fills Me with joy that you have come home. Now you can know Me as you never could before. You can know how near I am and hear the songs I've sung about you all along. Now we can walk together, and I can show you the places I've always wanted you to see. We can talk together and share our lives together. I've been here for you all along. It feels good to have you here with Me at last.

The One Who First Loved You,
>God

== == ==   == == == == == == == == ==

TRUST ME, NO MATTER WHAT

> If we are thrown into the blazing furnace, the God
> we serve is able to save us from it. . . . But even
> if he does not, we want you to know, O king,
> that we will not serve your gods.

Daniel   **3:17-18**

My Child,

>Once a king tried to force three young men to worship him, but they wouldn't do it. Why? I told them not to worship anyone but Me.

Well, the king got angry and decided to burn them to death. So the three young men told the king, "God is going to save us, but even if He doesn't, we're still going to obey Him." The end of the story is, I did save them. The point of the story is, they were willing to worship Me whether I saved them or not.

I'm still looking for young people who'll take a stand for Me like those three did. I'll know that you are truly intense about Me when you decide to obey Me, not because of what I can do for you, but simply because you love Me. I love you, too.

Your Deliverer,
>God

== == ==   == == == == == == == == ==

I AM THE RIVER

There is a river whose streams make glad the city of God, the holy place where the Most High dwells. God is within her, she will not fail.

Psalm 46:4-5

Dear Child,

>The kingdom of God is anywhere My Holy Spirit dwells. That means if you have trusted Me as your God and Jesus as your Savior, then the kingdom of God is in you! Running right down through the main street of your being, there is a river—an amazing, powerful, sparkling river of life. It is a river that makes you strong in a way you'll never be strengthened by taking vitamins, lifting weights, or running a triathlon. It's a river that sends spiritual strength throughout your entire personality to fill up your whole being.

So be aware of who you are in Me and Who I am in you. Your heart houses My Spirit, and I am the current of life that flows through you. Live in this reality, and nothing will knock you down!

The River,
>God

== == ==   == == == == == == == == ==

I'M TALKING TO YOU

Listen and hear my voice;
pay attention and hear what I say.

Isaiah 28:23

My Child,

>There is so much noise all around you: traffic, television, loud music in passing cars, babies crying, and people talking, shouting, or laughing. It's hard to hear your own thoughts, much less listen for My quiet voice.

I'm asking you to listen. I want to get a word in edgewise. I have personal words for your life—words of love, encouragement, and guidance. One of the best ways to hear from Me is by reading the Bible. Yes, the Bible. It's the bestseller that tops all bestseller lists. Begin in Mark or John. Before you read, ask My Holy Spirit to bring the words to life for you. Plug in your heart when you read, and you will hear Me. After you read, talk to Me. Ask Me anything you like. Then listen for My answer.

Your Friend,
>God

== == ==   == == == == == == == == ==

MIND YOUR STEP

Great peace have they who love your law,
and nothing can make them stumble.

| Psalm | 119:165 |

Dear Child,

>When you go hiking, would you rather wear sturdy hiking boots or slippery church shoes? Not a tough choice. With the boots, you can step anywhere. If you land in water, no problem—boots are waterproof. If you step on a thick root, no problem—boots absorb the shock. If you go hiking in slippery church shoes, you'll spend half your time falling down.

My Word is like hiking boots. Love My Word, obey it, and you'll be prepared to hike through life. You'll never have to worry about whether you're disobeying Me. You'll know what I want, you'll be doing it, and you can step wherever you like. People who hate My Word walk through life, slipping and sliding, never really sure whether they are right or wrong and always wondering if I'm mad at them. I love you either way, but you'll have a more enjoyable journey if you walk in the boots of My Word.

Your Traction,
>God

== == ==   == == == == == == == == ==

LOVE IN ACTION

This is how we know what love is: Jesus Christ
laid down his life for us. . . . And this is his command:
to believe in the name of his Son, Jesus Christ,
and to love one another as he commanded us.

1 John | **3:16-23**

Dear Child of Mine,

>Jesus was love in action. You can see My love just by looking at His life. He listened to people. He helped them, healed them, and gave them hope.

The most vivid picture of His love was His death on the cross. Nobody took Jesus' life. He gave it up for you. The best way to thank Him is to receive His love. Ask Him to love others through you. He'll do it!

Pick out some people who really look like they need His love. Don't try to love them with your own love. Let the love of Jesus take over in you. You'll be surprised at the kindness and caring that will come through you to others.

Your Loving Father,
>God

== == ==   == == == == == == == == ==

CLOSER THAN A PHONE CALL

**We do not know what to do,
but our eyes are upon you.**

| 2 Chronicles | 20:12 |

Dear Child,

>I know how confusing your life can seem at times. When you don't know what to do, wouldn't it be nice to have a little video game called Easy Answers? Just flip it on, and it tells you what you need to know. Maybe you'd like somebody wise and experienced sitting by the phone twenty-four hours a day with the right advice for each situation.

Life on this planet is not that simple. It's tough at times, but My book—the Bible—is full of answers. Read it. You'll see. My Son, Jesus, has walked ahead of you through the obstacle course called life. Keep your eyes on Him when you don't know what to do. Talk to Him every time you're confused. You'll find out He's even closer than your telephone. So am I.

Your Father,
>God

== == ==   == == == == == == == == ==

LET ME BE YOUR DEFENDER

Though I walk in the midst of trouble,
you preserve my life; you stretch out your
hand against the anger of my foes,
with your right hand you save Me.

| Psalm | 138: 7 |

My Child,

>It's a tough world out there. Believe Me, I know. Sometimes people or circumstances seem to gang up on you, and when they do, you may feel afraid. That's okay. I understand, and I care.

I want to help you cope with life. That's why I want you to call on Me. Tell Me your fears. I'll be right beside you in the midst of your struggles.

If I have to carry you, I will. I'll be your defender. I want to make a difference in your everyday life. So, don't be afraid.

Your Defender,
>God

== == ==   == == == == == == == == ==

I'M READING YOUR HEART

He has showed you, O man, what is good. And what does the LORD require of you? To act justly and to love mercy and to walk humbly with your God.

Micah   6:8

My Child,

>I created you to make a difference in the world. Does that mean I expect you to be elected president, head up a huge corporation, or spearhead a missionary effort? Those things are certainly possible, but you don't have to achieve big things to please Me.

I want you to live your life honestly, without a lot of fanfare. Respect other people, and treat them fairly. Show mercy and simple kindness as Jesus did. Walk with Me a day at a time. The movers and shakers of your society may rack up political and financial power, but I'm not impressed. I'm reading your heart, not your bankbook. Deeds of quiet humility are what earn interest in My kingdom.

The One Whose Will Is Perfect,
>God

== == ==   == == == == == == == == ==

THROW OUT THE CATALOG

What kind of deal is it to get everything you want but lose yourself? What could you ever trade your soul for.

Matthew 16:26 | THE MESSAGE

Dear Child of Mine,

>Suppose life was like a mail-order catalog, and you could just flip through the pages, selecting everything your heart desired: computers, cars, clothes, fancy vacations, fame, money, power—no limits.

Only the day your order was delivered, it came with a bill that said, "Payment required: Your eternal soul." Would you still place the order? Lots of people do, but they don't fully understand the trade they're making. To begin with, the catalog is a rip-off. It will never deliver in full anyway. Even if it did, no amount of stuff would ever satisfy your soul's restless longing for Me.

So throw out the world's catalog and open up the pages of My plan for you—the Bible. My love delivers what it promises!

Your Loving Dad,
>God

== == ==   == == == == == == == == ==

IT'S NOT RELIGION, IT'S A RELATIONSHIP

You can never please God without faith, without depending on him. Anyone who wants to come to God must believe that there is a God and that he rewards those who sincerely look for him.

Hebrews | **11:6 TLB**

Dear Child,

>It may surprise you to know that I'm not the slightest bit interested in religion—the traditions, buildings, and stained-glass windows. That's not what I'm about. What I want is for us to have a relationship—a friendship—where I can talk to you and you can talk to Me at anytime and about anything. You might be thinking that it's pretty hard to talk to somebody you can't even see. I know. That's where faith comes in.

Faith is believing in what you can't see. Faith is showing up in the early hours of the morning with your Bible in your lap, believing that I'll meet you there. The reward of faith is that when you show up believing I'll be there, I will! Don't miss out on the excitement of the faith adventure that's waiting for you when you learn to trust Me.

The Friend Who's Waiting,
>God

== == ==   == == == == == == == == ==

LET ME REFUEL YOUR LIFE

Hope does not disappoint us, because God has poured out his love into our hearts by the Holy Spirit, whom he has given us.

| Romans | 5:5 |

Dear Child,

>Trying to run your life without hope is like trying to run your car without gas; you won't get far. Sometimes it seems like the world has run out of hope. With all the hype and nonsense, people don't know what to believe in, so they don't believe in anything.

Some kids you know probably have learned to expect the worst. Maybe you've felt that way yourself. Well, even though it's easy to stop believing in other people and yourself, I can give you a reason to believe that your life is worth the effort—that the world is worth your best shot. Come and let Me refuel your life. Let Me fill you with hope. I've got plenty to spare!

The Hope that You Run On,
>God

== == == == == == == == == == == ==

IN THE MARKET FOR CONFIDENCE?

I am still confident of this: I will see the goodness of the LORD in the land of the living.

Psalm **27:13**

Dear Child,

>Have you ever noticed that some people just seem to have an air of confidence about them? What makes for real confidence? Is it looks or brains, money or clothes, or maybe popularity? It might surprise you to know that some of the people who look the most confident on the outside are really the most insecure. I know because I can read their thoughts. Inside, they're thinking, *I wonder what she thinks of me?* or, *Does this outfit make me look fat?* or, *What if I say the wrong thing?*

Real confidence comes from knowing Me, knowing that I love you unconditionally, and I'll never, ever let you down. A gut-level understanding of that reality will make you strong, confident, and steady as a rock. Believe Me.

Your Confidence,
>God

== == ==   == == == == == == == == ==

I'VE GOT A PLAN

**Many are the plans in a man's heart, but
it is the LORD's purpose that prevails.**

| Proverbs | 19:21 |

Dear Child,

>So many people get their spiritual lives turned around backwards.
With good intentions, they wake up every morning thinking, *Now,
what can I do for God today?* They use their creative energy to hatch
what they consider great plans for My kingdom. Then they roll up their
sleeves and start working feverishly to accomplish their own plans.
They never ask Me what I want. That's like your parents buying you
an expensive birthday present without once considering what you had
in mind.

You see, I have plans of My own I want to involve you in. So learn to
listen for My voice. Look around. Find out where I'm already at work
and join Me there. You will discover the excitement of working with
Me to bring My plans to completion.

The Ultimate Planner,
>God

== == ==   == == == == == == == == ==

WATCH HOW I DO IT

> "Walk with me and work with me—watch how I do it.
> Learn the unforced rhythms of grace. I won't lay
> anything heavy or ill-fitting on you. Keep company
> with me and you'll learn to live freely and lightly."

Matthew 11:29- | 30 THE MESSAGE

My Child,

>Some people will do everything they can to complicate the life of
faith. They'll try to strangle you with rules and trip you up with
regulations. They'll appoint themselves as watch dogs of your faith if
you let them.

Steer clear of those people! If you don't, they'll strip the beauty and
freedom out of your heart as quickly as I pour it in. The best way to
learn to travel the faith journey is to walk with Me. The surest way to
figure out how it works is to work with Me.

There is a freedom that you'll learn to put on every day—a freedom
tailor-made for you. There's a dance of grace so joyful it makes you
feel like you're flying. Watch and follow Me.

Love Always,
>God

== == ==   == == == == == == == == ==

HOW TO CHOOSE WELL

I will go to the king, even though it is against the law. And if I perish, I perish.

| | | | | | Esther | | 4:16 | | | | | |

Dear Child,

>Esther was a beautiful young Jewish woman who became the queen of Persia, but her husband, the king, didn't know she was Jewish. Esther found out that an evil man named Haman was plotting to have all the Jews in the land put to death. She knew she had to tell the king about the plot, but the penalty for approaching the king without being summoned was death. Here was Esther's dilemma: Should she risk death to save her people, or should she save her own neck and let them die? Esther saved her people, and her own life was spared.

Like Esther, you'll have some important choices to make in your life—choices that may be risky. Come to Me when you need the wisdom and courage to choose well.

Your Counselor,
>God

== == ==   == == == == == == == == ==

SH-H-H-H, SLOW DOWN

This is what the Sovereign Lᴏʀᴅ, the Holy One of Israel, says: "In repentance and rest is your salvation, in quietness and trust is your strength."

| Isaiah | 30:15 |

Dear Child of Mine,

>Repentance is just a fancy word that means "to turn around." It literally means "to change your mind."

My advice is to change your mind about all the busyness in your life. Most people think the more they plan and the more they do, the safer and stronger they will be. I see it differently. I want you to slow down and take time to be quiet. Rest and trust Me, and I'll help you to be strong and successful anyway. That doesn't mean that you never have to plan or take action, but it does mean that if all you do is plan and try, you're missing out on My best for you.

Taking time out to be with Me during a busy day is always a good idea. As you wait on Me, I'll give you the strength you need. Slow down a little!

Your Advisor,
>God

== == ==   == == == == == == == == ==

THE HOPE OF THE WORLD

**Heal the sick, raise the dead, cleanse those
who have leprosy, drive out demons.
Freely you have received, freely give.**

Matthew 10:8

My Child,

>The world is a broken place full of hurting people and seemingly
hopeless situations. This is not the way I created it, but since man fell
from the grace I provided in the beginning, all kinds of brokenness
(suffering, sorrow, poverty, pain, and death) came into the world.

Through Jesus Christ, there is hope for restoration in the midst of all
the brokenness. Because you follow Jesus, now you are the hope of
the world. You are the hands and feet and heart of Christ on earth.
The heart of Christ does not give up. It sacrifices everything it has to
reach out and heal the world.

Don't be discouraged by what seem to be overwhelming odds. You
can't save the world by yourself, and you can't do it in a day. You can
do your part. With my Spirit in you, you can make a difference—one
heart, one life, one day, one person, one challenge at a time.

Your Hope,
>God

== == ==   == == == == == == == == ==

LIKE MONEY IN THE BANK

He will keep in perfect peace all those who trust in him, whose thoughts turn often to the Lord!

Isaiah 26:3 TLB

Dear Child,

>Every time you take your thoughts off of your worries and turn them to Me, you're depositing peace into your spiritual bank. Every time you use your energy for trusting Me instead of wasting it on fretting, you're adding more peace to your spiritual bank account. Your trusting thoughts of Me remind you that I'm in control. No matter what is troubling you, I am more powerful. No matter what is worrying you, My love is greater.

As you continue to deposit your trusting thoughts of Me into your spiritual bank, they will gather interest and grow. Pretty soon, you will have a huge treasure of peace to draw on when stressful situations spring up. So think of Me often and trust in Me. I won't disappoint you.

Your Peace Giver,
>God

== == ==   == == == == == == == == ==

LET'S TALK TODAY

**Before they call I will answer; while
they are still speaking I will hear.**

| Isaiah | 65:24 |

Dear Child,

>Prayer is not a process of trying to talk Me into doing something that I don't want to do. Prayer is realizing how willing I am to be involved in your life and how excited I am about involving you in Mine.

The moment you admit in prayer that you've been wrong, I forgive you. In prayer, I can encourage you when you're down and show you the way when you're lost. I can give you courage to face your fears, and I can bend down to dry your tears.

Can't you tell by now how much I want to talk with you? In fact, I'm listening for your prayers day and night. I'm already answering your call while it's still just a thought in your head! Let's talk today.

Your Friend Who Listens,
>God

== == ==   == == == == == == == == ==

UNWRAP YOUR GIFTS

Do not throw away your confidence, which has a great reward. For you have need of endurance, so that when you have done the will of God, you may receive what was promised.

Hebrews 10:35-36 NASB

Dear Child,

>You are like a little kid on Christmas morning who has barely begun to unwrap his gifts. One of the most precious gifts under the tree is still wrapped. It's the gift of confidence. It's a gift that is valuable not only for itself, but because it comes with an added bonus. Just like a pizza with a coupon taped to the box that's good for a free order of bread sticks, you can redeem the coupon on your box of confidence for the added gift of endurance.

Endurance is the gift of keeping on going even when the going gets tough. Trust Me, keeping on in the Christian life is what leads to the real rewards! So start unwrapping your gifts, and don't throw your confidence out with the wrapping paper! You're going to need it.

The Gift Giver,
>God

== == ==   == == == == == == == == ==

PUT YOUR BOARD IN THE WATER

What good is it, my brothers, if a man claims to have faith but has no deeds? Can such faith save him?

| | | James | | 2:14 | | |

My Child,

>Suppose someone gives you a top-of-the-line surfboard and a manual on surfing. On day one, you read all about the board itself and how it's made. On day two, you read about the techniques of surfing. On day three, you read about safety in surfing and the history of surfing in the United States. For months you study the manual. You spend hours at the beach watching others on their surfboards. If you never put your board in the water and feel the thrill of riding a wave, what's the point? You might as well not have a board at all.

The same is true of your faith. You can read and believe everything about Me, but if you never put your faith into action, what good is it to either of us? So, how about it? Surf's up!

The Lord of Faith *and* Deeds,
>God

== == == == == == == == == == == ==

AN ADDED BONUS

That's my parting gift to you. Peace.
I don't leave you the way you're used
to being left. . . . So don't be upset.

| John 14:27 | THE MESSAGE |

My Child,

>Most people live with chaos and conflict in their lives: outside
conflicts with other people and situations, and inside conflicts
between different opinions and ideas in their own heads.

Jesus wants to give you peace. When you receive His love, His
peace is an added bonus. When you embrace His friendship, you'll
be able to set Him, like the sun, in the center of your personal solar
system. Then all of the chaotic struggles and conflicts tend to quiet
down. All of the questions untangle themselves. All of the things you
care about line up and revolve around Jesus, like planets pulled into
the orbit of His grace. And He will give you peace.

Peace Always,
>God

== == ==   == == == == == == == == ==

GAME OVER

**What I mean, brothers, is that the time is short. . . .
For this world in its present form is passing away.**

| 1 Corinthians | 7:29–31 |

My Child,

>Believe it or not, the world is going to end. I'm not some crazy street preacher yelling, "The end is near." I'm God. In My Bible I'm saying, "Time is short. The end is near." Were you thinking about messing around with sex, drinking, or partying for a little while? Were you planning on getting serious about Me later? There's no time for that.

I've created you to do great things—things that are going to bless you and others—things that are going to make the world a better place. I'm waiting on you to get real with Me. I'm looking for anyone crazy enough to do it My way—not tomorrow, but now. Are you in or out? If you think your life doesn't matter, you're wrong. No one else can do what I have for you to do. This is not a game. It's real, and we're running out of time.

Your Motivator,
>God

== == ==   == == == == == == == == ==

I LOVE YOU FOREVER

Though the mountains be shaken and the hills be removed, yet my unfailing love for you will not be shaken nor my covenant of peace be removed," says the LORD, who has compassion on you.

| Isaiah | 54:10 |

Dear Child,

>I have chosen you to be Mine. I want to have a relationship with you. Even if you turn from Me—even if you hate Me—I will still love you.

Your attitude and behavior don't change My love for you. If you turn from Me, or cut yourself off from Me, I still want to be with you. It's like when you turn off the faucet. Does the water just disappear out of the pipe? No, it stays there waiting for you to turn on the faucet again. I'm like that water. I'm here waiting. I want you as My child. No disobedience or rebellion on your part can change that.

I have chosen you, and I will never reject you. Please don't cut yourself off from My love.

Your Faithful Father,
>God

== == ==   == == == == == == == == ==

CLONINGER

WAS JESUS SURPRISED?

Jesus . . . knew mankind to the core.

| John | 2:24 TLB |

Dear Child,

>Jesus had every reason to be disillusioned by the people around Him. The Pharisees were jealous of His popularity; the Romans were suspicious of His power. In His hometown, people gave Him no respect. On the road, some people followed Him just because they thought His miracles were cool. Even His best friends let Him down. They swore they'd never betray Him, but when push came to shove, they all bailed, and Jesus was alone.

Was He surprised? Not in the least. He understood human nature for two reasons. To begin with, He was a human being and part of the human family. He still is. The other reason is that He was with Me when I created human beings. Your weakness never surprises Him. He knows you as you are, and He loves you anyway. So do I.

Your Loving Father,
>God

== == ==   == == == == == == == == ==

I WILL MEET ALL YOUR NEEDS

**I have learned to be content whatever the circumstances. . . .
I can do everything through him who gives me strength.**

| Philippians | 4:11-13 |

Dear Child,

>Contentment is a valuable commodity. Some people have boats, cars, big houses, and money, but they can't find contentment. What good is all that stuff if they aren't satisfied with it?

Contentment is something that only I can give. Paul, one of My children, spent a lot of his life in jail. Even there, Paul was content because he knew this truth: "Jesus gives me all I need." Despite his circumstances, Paul knew that Jesus would take care of him.

Trust Me to meet your needs, and you will always be content. Only I can meet your needs . . . and I will.

The Giver of Contentment,
>God

== == ==   == == == == == == == == ==

BE PREPARED

Put on the full armor of God so that you can take your
stand against the devil's schemes. For our struggle is not
against flesh and blood, but against the rulers, against the
authorities, against the powers of this dark world and against
the spiritual forces of evil in the heavenly realms.

Ephesians 6:11-12

Dear Child,

>What kind of general would send his soldiers into battle with no
weapons, no strategy, and no information about enemy operations?
He would either be cruel or stupid. Trust Me, I am neither. As your
Commander in Chief, I want you to be prepared. Life on planet Earth
is quite literally a daily battle, but it's spiritual, not physical. It's a battle
between good and evil, right and wrong, truth and lies. You will need
My armor to stand against the enemy. So put on the helmet of
salvation, the belt of truth, the breastplate of right living, and the
shoes of good news. Take up the shield of faith and the sword of the
Spirit. Get in the habit of praying effortlessly and trustingly. Now,
follow Me!

Your General,
>God

== == ==   == == == == == == == == ==

REFERENCES

ABOUT THE AUTHORS

Claire Cloninger, winner of four Dove Awards for songwriting, also created the phenomenally successful musical *My Utmost for His Highest*. She has authored nine books, including best-sellers *A Place Called Simplicity* and *Dear Abba*.

Curt Cloninger, Claire's son, is employed as the Internet Administrator for Integrity Music and is the worship leader at the Mobile Vineyard Christian Fellowship. He spent two years in Youth With a Mission and has worked as a middle-school teacher, a high-school track coach, and a house parent in a children's home. He and his wife, Julie, are parents of a daughter, Caroline.

If you have enjoyed this book, or if it has
impacted your life, we would like to hear from you.

Please contact us at:

RiverOak Publishing
Department E
P.O. Box 700143
Tulsa, OK 74170-0143

Additional copies of this book
and other titles in the *E-mail from God* series
are available from your local bookstore.

E-mail from God for Teens

More E-mail from God for Teens

E-mail from God for Men

E-mail from God for Women

E-mail from God for Kids

E-mail from God for Teens screensaver

RIVER
OAK
PUBLISHING